frederick wight
visions of california

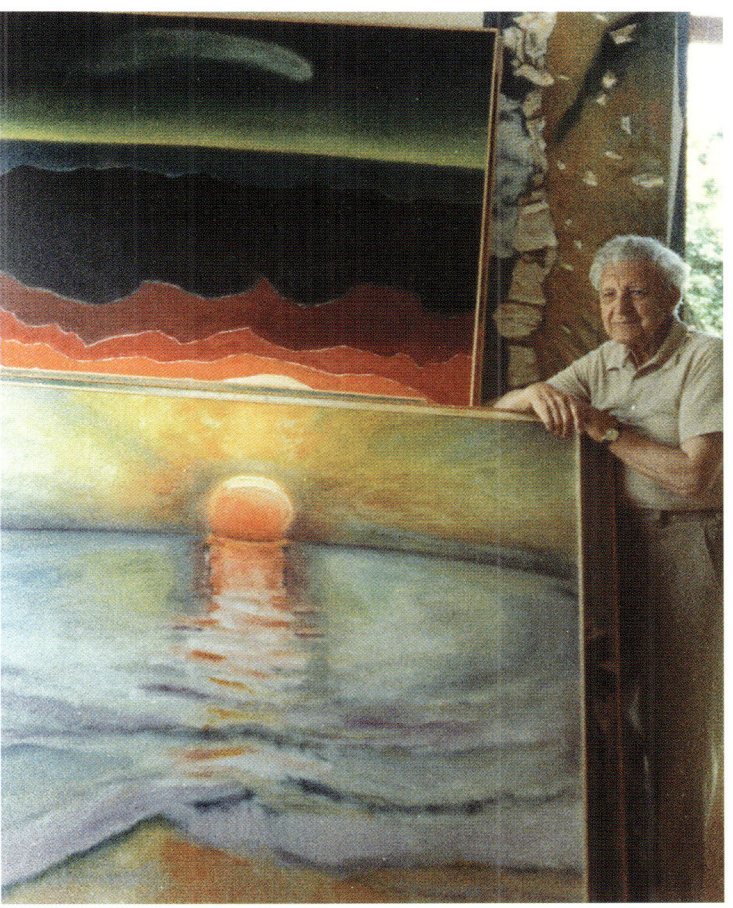

Frederick Wight, 1984

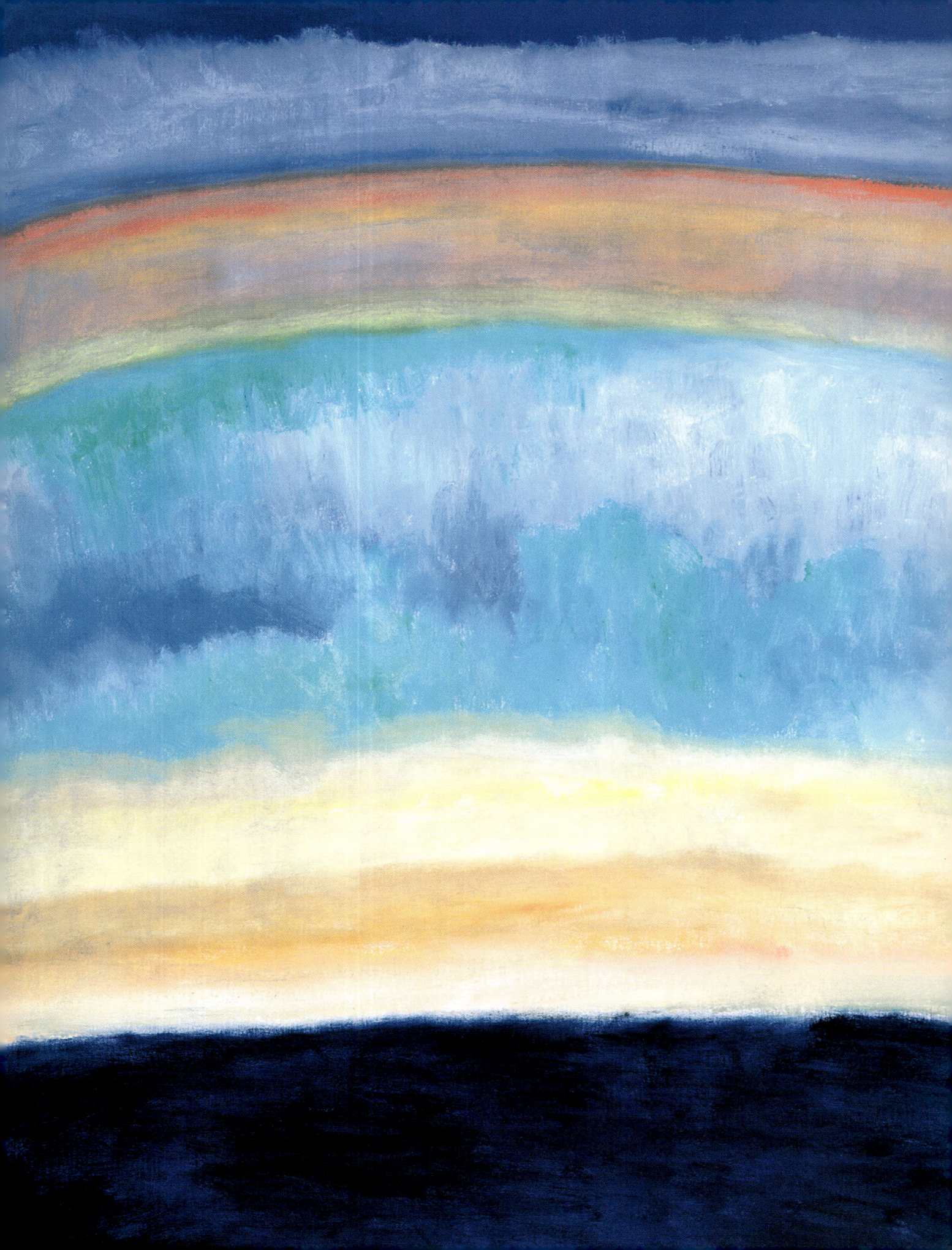

frederick wight
visions of california

april 16 - may 28 2005

louis stern fine arts
9002 melrose avenue   west hollywood, CA 90069
t 310-276-0147 f 310-276-7740   gallery@louisstern.com
www.louissternfinearts.com

acknowledgement
louis stern 9

appreciation
henry t. hopkins 10

essay
susan c. larsen 13

color plates 17

chronology 86

selected solo exhibitions 88

selected group exhibitions 89

collections 91

exhibition checklist 92

selected bibliography 94

Frederick Wight's luminescent California-centric paintings have long been of interest to me, especially those executed during the last decade of his life. Initially Wight's oils seemed closely related to the work of his friend and colleague Georgia O'Keefe and the earlier, symbol-laden compositions of Arthur Dove. But in preparing this exhibition, I have come to appreciate Wight's dreamily composed visions of the natural world as entirely unique.

In the past, Wight has been revered in the Los Angeles art community for his extraordinary contributions as an educator and curator. With this exhibition, in keeping with my commitment to re-invigorate interest in the groundbreaking work of mid-twentieth century California painters, I hope to inspire a kindred respect for his work as an artist.

First and foremost, I am indebted to the artist's son, George Wight. This exhibition came to be in large part due to George's patience, energy and passion for the work and for his father's legacy. His willingness to forage through archival information, imagery and even memory has been a great inspiration to me.

I also want to express a personal thank you to Joan Wight. She has been unfailingly gracious with our every request and entirely supportive of our efforts to organize this exhibition of her husband's work.

Joni Gordon of Newspace Gallery has provided invaluable assistance in our seemingly endless search for documentation. Her personal recollections and her generosity in articulating them have made this endeavor infinitely easier.

I would also like to thank Henry Hopkins and Susan Larsen for their literary contributions.

Finally, without the yeoman efforts of my staff, Jennifer Ward, Marie Chambers and Deborah Stern, this publication simply would not exist. I am deeply appreciative of their individual contributions to this project and extend to them all my sincerest thanks.

Louis Stern

henry t. hopkins

It is my great pleasure to write a few words about my extended friendship with Frederick Wight. He was my mentor during my study of modern art history at UCLA in the late 1950's and remained my mentor throughout much of my professional career as a museum director and teacher.

First, let me describe him. In his mid-fifties, he was rather tall despite being slightly stooped. His hair was wavy and flecked with gray. His face bore the handsome angularity of a second-generation Yankee softened by well-earned wrinkles. His eyes were sharp, highly perceptive. His voice was full and pleasantly enhanced with a slight stammer. This trademark stammer became especially noticeable as he awaited reaction to one of his wry stories. He always wore a shirt, tie and jacket, the latter of which being somewhat wrinkled as if to signify his profession. Even after long association, he was addressed as Mr. Wight, never Fred.

When we first met in 1957 he was teaching a course in Twentieth-Century art to large and appreciative undergraduate classes in UCLA's fledgling art history department. He was also chair of the department that encompassed not only art history but art practice as well. He was also director of the UCLA art galleries. This should give you some sense of his broad capabilities and energy. He was a marvelous teacher who saw art not only through the eyes of history and culture but also through the eyes of a practicing artist, a great rarity in those days.

He was probably most admired for his handling of the UCLA art galleries. There he curated, wrote about and mounted extraordinary exhibitions of Twentieth Century Art. His were exhibitions that put the other local professional museums to shame. He fed the art-starved Los Angeles community with such treats as Jean Arp, Charles Sheeler, John Marin, Morris Graves, Hans Hoffmann, Bradley Walker Tomlin, Arthur Dove, Richard Neutra, Henri Matisse, Amedeo Modigliani, and Pablo Picasso. He was also instrumental in the establishment of the Grunwald Center for the Graphic Arts and the Franklin Murphy Sculpture Garden at UCLA. How he managed to do this on a modest university budget was a mystery. The strong art council that he had founded served as a vital support for his efforts. The council was ramrodded by Mrs. Sidney F. "Francie" Brody who became the living symbol of John Mortimer's "She who must be obeyed." Upon his retirement in 1972 the gallery was re-named the Frederick S. Wight Art Gallery in his honor.

Our close association began in 1960 when I had to choose a topic for my doctoral dissertation. I asked Mr. Wight to chair my committee and he agreed to do so. I proposed doing an in-depth study of the "modernist" Los Angeles art scene from the 1930's until the present. The committee

Not willing to yield, I made the point that even though I was studying art history, I had been trained as a painter at the Art Institute of Chicago. Furthermore I argued that I was interested in the "real" art object rather than slides or books. This argument didn't impress anyone except Fred Wight. As a painter, he understood my thinking and convinced the rest of my team to let me try it. He gave me immediate support through his many contacts. He introduced me to artists Stanton MacDonald-Wright, Lorser Feitelson and Helen Lundeberg, dealers Frank Perls, Paul Kantor and Felix Landau and the collector Vincent Price.

With Fred Wight's considerable help and guidance I uncovered a world of rather wonderful events that had gone largely undocumented in the national art press. For example, LA had had a showing of *Guernica* and Duchamp's *Nude Descending a Staircase* at the Stendhal Gallery, the great Arensberg Collection and Galka Scheyer and the *Blue Four*, the Post-Surrealist movement at the Vincent Price Gallery of Modern Art and William Copley's Surrealist Gallery.

After a year of research I approached my committee with a new concept. Since the UCLA art galleries had become such an important part of the Los Angeles art scene, why not do an exhibition of my research rather than a dissertation? Shock and awe was the response. Again, Fred Wight, a true museum man at heart, gave me the support that I needed. After all, he had studied at the Harvard Fogg Art Museum under the great Paul Sachs who had made Harvard the training ground for future art museum directors.

Thus my first exhibition, entitled "Fifty Paintings by Thirty-Seven Painters of the Los Angeles Area," came to fruition on March 20, 1960, complete with catalogue. Henry Seldis, art critic for the Los Angeles Times, pointed out that this was the first time in the history of any major university that such a privilege had been granted to a graduate student. As Fred Wight was a master at getting UCLA exhibitions shown at other institutions, my show traveled to the Dallas Musuem of Contemporary Art, the Des Moines Art Center, San Antonio's McNay Institute, the Museum of New Mexico, the Roswell Art Museum, the San Francisco Museum of Art and the Seattle Art Museum. How can one ever thank someone enough for that type of support and belief?

To Fred Wight's great credit, that exhibition led directly to my employment at the Los Angeles County Museum in 1961 and ultimately to my forty-year career as an art museum professional.

It would be remiss for me to end this essay without mentioning the other UCLA graduate students, friends and peers who were also mentored by Fred Wight. Many went on to brilliant art museum careers. James Demetrion directed the Hirschhorn Museum in Washington D.C. Walter Hopps co-founded the brilliant Menil Collection in Houston. Martin Friedman flourished at the Walker Art Center in Minneapolis. Due to Fred Wight, UCLA, for that moment, supplanted Harvard as the premiere training ground for museum directors.

Frederick Stallknect Wight was an extraordinary teacher, administrator and artist. This exhibition will attest to his considerable artistic powers. But to those of us who worked with him over the years, he was something even more remarkable: he was our believer.

Henry T. Hopkins
Professor Emeritus, UCLA

Henry T. Hopkins is a former museum director and educator and is currently Professor Emeritus in the Department of Art at the University of California, Los Angeles.

susan c. larsen

Frederick S. Wight moved from Boston to Los Angeles in 1953 to teach painting and to direct the art gallery of the University of California, Los Angeles. One wonders if the Los Angeles art community had any idea of its great good fortune to receive a person of such wide-ranging abilities, freshness of outlook and persuasive power. He was adept at the grand art of measure and balance. He valued the clairvoyant freedom of modern art but based his own creativity upon lived personal experience. He got along famously with artists even while working as a rigorous and eloquent critic. He courted and educated important donors to the UCLA gallery so that he could lay the riches of the art world before the artists, students and average folk of the city. He had a penetrating, spare writing style that contained a world of feeling and sincere belief in the power of art. Frederick Wight was a most unusual man who came to Los Angeles at just the right moment.

In the early fifties, Los Angeles stirred with a rare energy brought about by postwar prosperity, confidence in its regional mastery of advanced technology and a youthful culture acting as a magnet for creative spirits from all other parts of the country. Rich in talent, energy and individuality, the city's art institutions occasionally offered excellent exhibitions and but had thin permanent collections. The museum scene lacked system, rigor and most of all the depth that scholarship, intellectual vitality and critical acumen can bring to an institution and its programs.

Frederick Wight brought with him an elegant educational background and the spirit of purposeful creativity. His father had been a professor of classics at Johns Hopkins University and his mother an admired and successful regional artist. Frederick Wight was born in New York City in 1902 and grew up in the town of Chatham, Cape Cod. His early impressions of the world were primarily rural and his early attempts at written personal expression were rooted in American small town life. He went to the University of Virginia in Charlottesville where his devotion to painting and writing lent a firm direction to his studies. After graduation, he traveled to Paris for two years at the Academie Julien. Living in Paris in the mid-1920s, Wight reveled in the bohemian life of an art student, focusing upon his own work and a young man's exploration of independent experience. By his own admission, he paid little heed to exhibitions by many of the European modernists he would later study and admire.

In 1925, returning to the United States, he settled in Cape Cod to paint while also pursuing a writing career. His visual style is inflected with modernism but focuses upon regional subject matter: ship's captains, local folk, marine landscapes and studies of flora and fauna. Many years later, in Wight's novel, *Kindling* (1951), he would depict a Cape Cod village full of "primitive American desolation, loneliness and hope."[1]

He had modest success as a painter but more encouragement for his writing, which began to appear in such celebrated journals as *Colliers* and *The Saturday Evening Post* by the mid 1930s. The publication of his novel, *South*, in 1935 placed him among the rising generation of American regionalist writers. It was followed by *The Chronicle of Aaron Kane* (1936) and *Youth in Trust* in 1937.

Marriage to Joan Bingham in 1936 took the couple to her native England and throughout Europe for two years in 1937 and 1938. Their son, George Frederick Wight, was born in 1942 in Massachusetts where his father was already pursuing a promising career as a novelist and painter. Of course, World War II intervened and Frederick Wight left for service in the Navy where he served with distinction as a writer, linguist, translator and officer in the Office of Strategic Services.

Upon his return from the war in 1945, new opportunities beckoned. The G.I. Bill of Rights enabled Frederick Wight to enroll at Harvard University to study museum administration under the eminent professor, Paul Sachs. Many of the nation's great and influential museum directors had already graduated from Sach's uniquely successful program. Blending theory and practice, Sachs fostered creativity and taught social skills and bold leadership to his students. He supplied the scholarly background and inspired the will to make art live in their communities and on museum walls. In Frederick Wight, Sachs must have found a mature creative personality. Wight had the verbal skills to convey complexities of mind and spirit. Upon graduation, Sachs recommended him to Director James Plaut for the post of associate director at Boston's Institute of Contemporary Art. It was a highly successful appointment and Wight stayed six years, producing exhibitions of the work of Walter Gropius, Le Corbusier, Jacques Villon, Lyonel Feininger, Karl Zerbe, Hyman Bloom and many contemporary Bostonians.

When Frederick Wight accepted the directorship of the University of California, Los Angeles art galleries he did so as both museum professional and as a respected painter. Settling in Los Angeles with his family in 1953, he set a course that would change the artistic life of the city. His ability to conceive of important exhibitions and fund them made the UCLA art galleries a venue of the first importance. Wight was one of the few major intellects of his generation to focus his attention on American modernist painting. He wrote a wonderful book on Arthur Dove and created a retrospective exhibition of the artist's work in 1958. He saw the innovative power of the art of John Marin and celebrated that pioneer American modernist with an exhibition at the UCLA art gallery in 1955. Frederick Wight described Morris Graves as "a poet in paint"[2] when few people knew the true merit of this West Coast master. In 1956, Wight staged a Morris Graves exhibition and in the same year created "Contemporary Calligraphy: John Marin; Mark Tobey; Morris Graves."

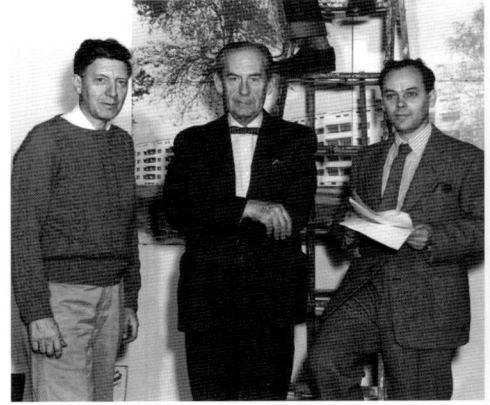
Frederick Wight, Walter Gropius, György Képes working on Gropius show at ICA Boston about 1950

In 1954, shortly after assuming his position at UCLA, Wight published a monograph on the Spanish master Francisco Goya. Wight's grasp of the importance of European modernism to American artists and audiences led him to create retrospective exhibitions featuring the art of: Hans Hofmann (1957); Richard Neutra (1958); Pablo Picasso (1961); Jacques Lipchitz (1963); Henri Matisse (1966); Alexander Archipenko (1967); Jean Arp (1968); Gerhard Marcks (1969). He also curated a retrospective of the work of Amadeo Modigliani for the Los Angeles County Museum of Art and wrote a romantic novel based on the artist's life in 1956.[3]

Wight was daring and masterful in his staging and scholarship as he engaged the public of Los Angeles. He retained the friendship and admiration of the artistic community of city, in itself an enviable achievement. He was truly responsible for the artistic education of the public of Los Angeles for over twenty years.

All the while, however, a quiet, private and important part of Wight's character flourished and revealed itself through his paintings. His closest friends were artists and they considered him as one of their community and fraternity. UCLA colleague William Brice said of his friend, Frederick Wight, "Fred was both public and private. It is in Fred's painting that we have a most direct view of his inner nature. . . visionary, reverent and mystical."[4] At Wight's memorial service in 1986, longtime friend Richard Diebenkorn described his colleague's public face as sometimes, "withering and iconoclastic." Diebenkorn continued, "He cared about us and he cared about our loving him. . . He was a complex and ambivalent character. This of course is what a painter needs to be."[5]

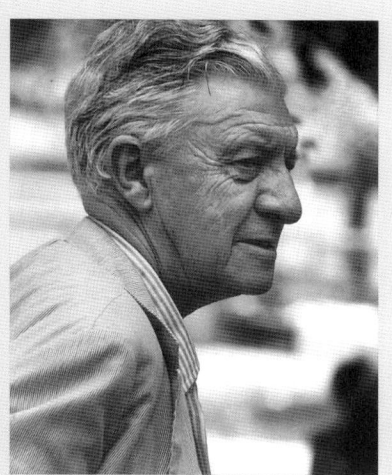

Frederick Wight, 1973

The paintings in our current exhibition come from a special period in the life of Frederick Wight. He retired from UCLA in 1973, an event that marked the onset of his creative fulfillment as a painter. It would have been easy for Frederick Wight to find and follow the latest stylistic trends in Los Angeles. He had helped to define the city as an international artistic center of innovation and excitement. It is clear that Wight's understanding of his calling went deeper than that. His paintings had to be nothing less than a full consideration of his place in the cosmos and in his own backyard. They had to be a fulfillment of an inner voice, something beyond style or politics or current events.

His mature paintings are filled with nature's most dramatic players: mountains; oceans; the moon and stars; the sun in its daily passage through space and time; palm trees; flowering plants; the desert landscape; his own patio garden filled with sunspots after rain. While others painted the human landscape of billboards, roads, messages, people and form itself, Wight celebrated the eternal elements of nature. Many years before, in his writings on Arthur Dove, Wight said of that congenial painter, "His paintings were abstractions drawn from the great events of nature. . . he kept his canvases small and his effects large enough to fill the sky."[6] Wight's paintings reveal his profoundly romantic character. In his paintings we sense his fixation upon time and mortality. In them, he reveals a transcendent mind that dealt with so many weighty and worldly things for so many years, but always kept its focus upon the heartbeat of nature in an average day.

As many of his friends discerned, Wight had an ironical sense of humor and a stern sense of truth. He often painted the giant towering palm trees of Los Angeles and even more often those of the desert near Palm Springs and Monte Rosa. The palm is now an archetypal image of southern California, mysterious and awkwardly humorous, prehistoric and wild. Many of our most prominent artists have used the palm tree as a multivalent emblem of the good life under the sun.

Wight's *Three Palms*, 1975 (plate 1), *Two Palms, Evening II*, 1977 (plate 5) and *Palm Dusk*, 1978 (plate 6) restore the trees to nature's keeping. Wight's palms soar and waver in the wind and heat. They are ringed by withered fronds and stand alternately as beacons and dusky silhouettes in the sun and the fading light. They have a vulnerable and friendly aspect despite their giant scale and commanding presence. They are returned to the great American landscape tradition, rescued in the nick of time from the life-draining grip of pop culture.

Suddenly Afternoon, 1979 (plate 12) is an emblematic painting with a single palm tree at its center. Surely a man as sophisticated as Frederick Wight knew he was breaking a central taboo of pictorial composition and also evoking precedents such as the vertical "zip" lines employed by Barnett Newman. Wight's well-groomed palm stands against a sunlight sky filled with glorious refracted light as luminous as in a stained glass panel. It is a halcyon moment in life, full, exultant, poignant in its self-conscious understanding of the inevitable passage of one moment into another.

Short Night, 1979 (plate 10) is a scene of drama and glamour within nature's lexicon. A palm stands as a smoky presence in the middle swiftly rising mountains. It is all lit up by nature as if by fireworks, glowing, gorgeous and real.

In *Desert Morning (Morning Hours II)*, 1981 (plate 17), Wight savors the slow breaking of the light over a desert landscape. In exquisite balance for just a few minutes, the fading moon greets the morning sun.

Frederick Wight's early appreciation of American painters, John Marin, Arthur Dove, and Marsden Hartley resonates in his marine paintings of the mid-1980s. *Returning Day*, 1982 (plate 20) juxtaposes a restless sea with an inky blue sky pierced by the rising sun. It has something of the mystery and wild energy of a work by Ryder. *Eclipse*, 1984 (plate 33) could only be painted by one who had spent a lifetime gazing out at the Pacific Ocean and marveling at incandescent sunsets lending a wild grandeur to an endless horizon.

These would be remarkable paintings even if we were to assume that Frederick Wight traveled around southern California in search of unique moments of unusual cosmic alignments and wondrous views. Of course, his rigorous mind would not allow such an easy strategy even if it yielded felicitous results. Light as an agent of physical motion and temporal passage must be active everywhere and always, if it is to have a metaphysical dimension for the human mind. He found similar inspiration in his own garden drenched with a radiance that seems otherworldly. *Garden*, 1984 (plate 30) and *Garden II*, 1984 (plate 32) are alive with the vibration of energy and light. They glow with a transcendental spirit akin to that of the earliest paintings of Kandinsky and the Blue Rider group. It is clear that Frederick Wight saw the world as wholly alive, each living thing a part of a vibrant universe.

Meditation on Mating, 1984 (plate 34) gives a wry nod to the inevitable loneliness of individuals even as they come together in love. Two spectral illuminations hover over the water in harmonic union, supporting one another in a moment that will soon melt into another. *School of Clouds*, 1984 (plate 35) is a buoyant image with clouds that suggest a school of fish swimming in the sky. Frederick Wight did admire much abstract painting but his writings reveal a personality that found little of import in art which was wholly divorced from nature. *Band*, 1986 (plate 39) takes his pictorial vocabulary to the edge of abstraction which was exactly the horizon he preferred to maintain.

Wight's journey to Los Angeles in 1953 was a fateful one for him and for the cultural history of the city. He found his own best landscape as a painter and a lifetime of distinguished achievement as a curator, director and writer. How fortunate it was that at an early time in the city's artistic development, a person so versatile, big-hearted and wise came to work at its most important institution of higher education. He established a spirited and friendly discourse between artists and writers. He showed us all how great it can be to keep one's creative life as generous and broad and filled with wonder as we can.

Susan C. Larsen, Ph.D.

1 Frederick Wight. **Kindling**, (Boston: Little Brown and Company, 1951), p. 31.
2 Frederick S. Wight. **The Potent Image: Art in the Western World from Cave Paintings to the 1970s**, (New York: Collier Books, 1976), p. 475.
3 Frederick Wight. **The Verge of Glory**, (New York: Harcourt, Brace and Company, 1956).
4 "In Memoriam, Frederick S. Wight, Art: Los Angeles," University of California, Los Angeles, 1986, p. 2.
5 Ibid.
6 Frederick S. Wight, **The Potent Image**, p. 445.

Susan C. Larsen is currently Collector, New England Region for the Archives of American Art, Smithsonian Institution. She was formerly Professor of Art History at the University of Southern California and Curator of the Permanent Collection at the Whitney Museum of American Art in New York City. She lives in coastal Maine.

plates

1 **three palms**

march 1975

oil on canvas

96 x 43 inches

243.8 x 109.2 centimeters

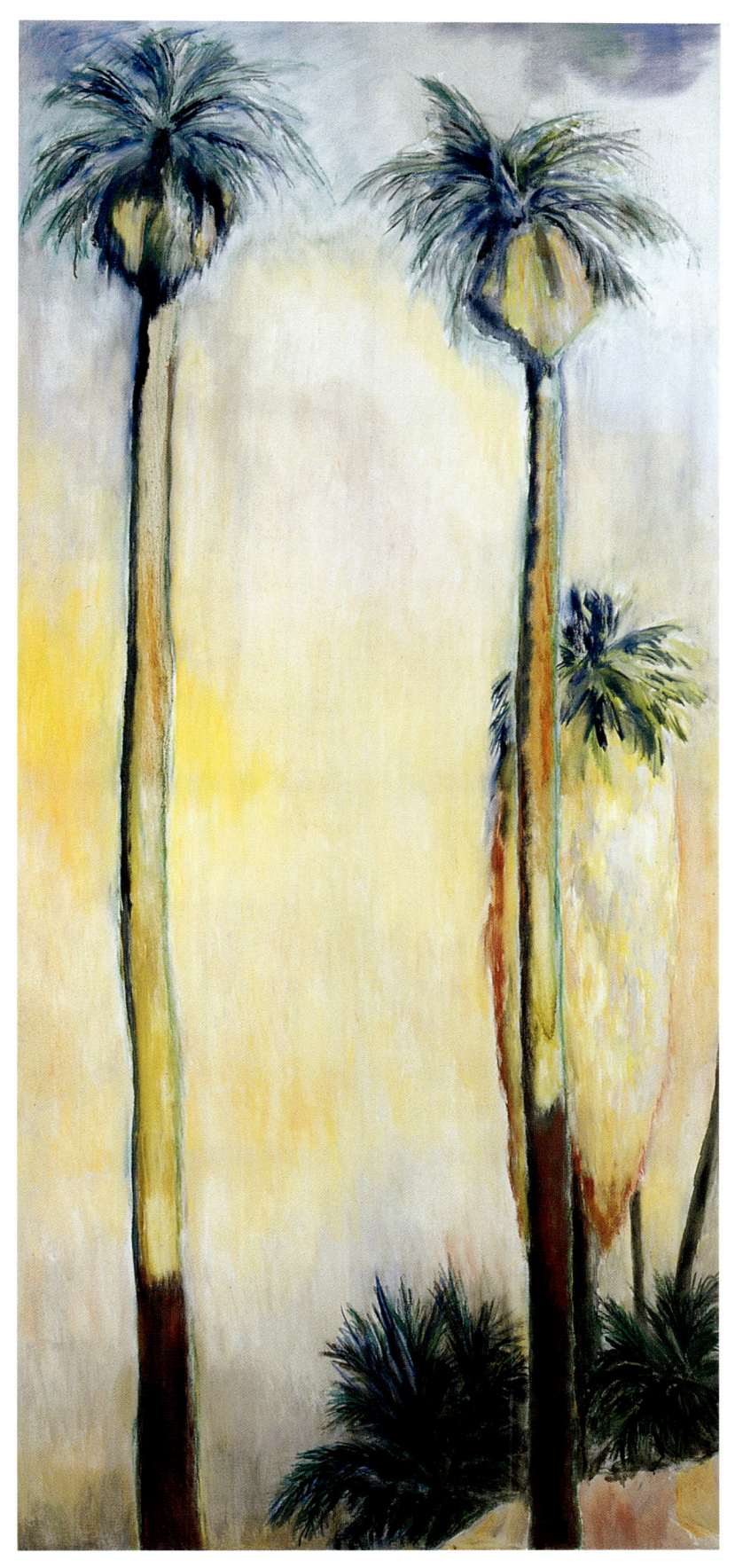

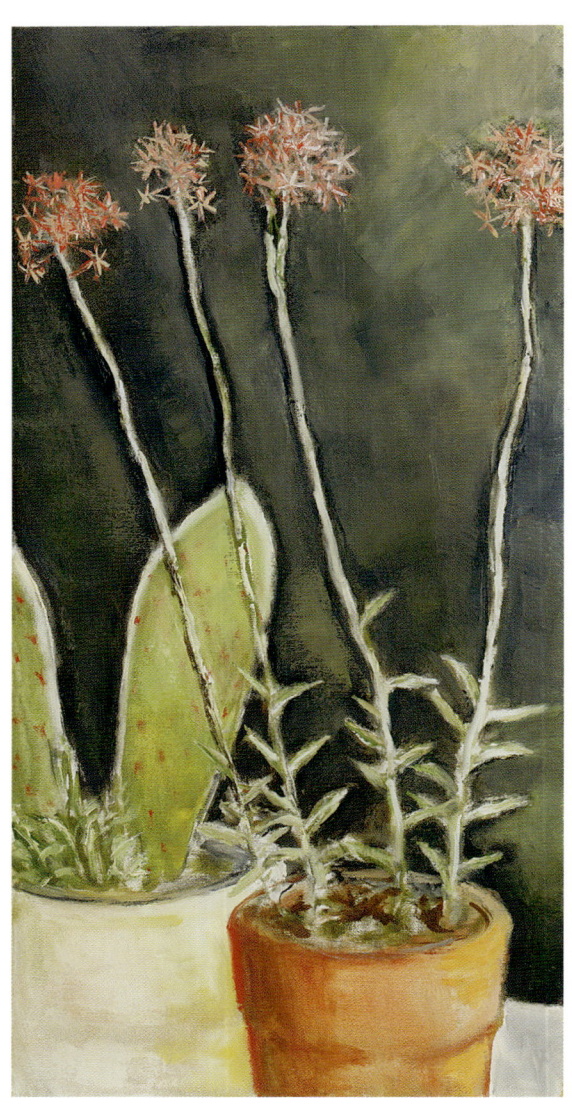

2 orchid catcus

december 1975

oil on canvas

30 x 15 inches

76.2 x 38.1 centimeters

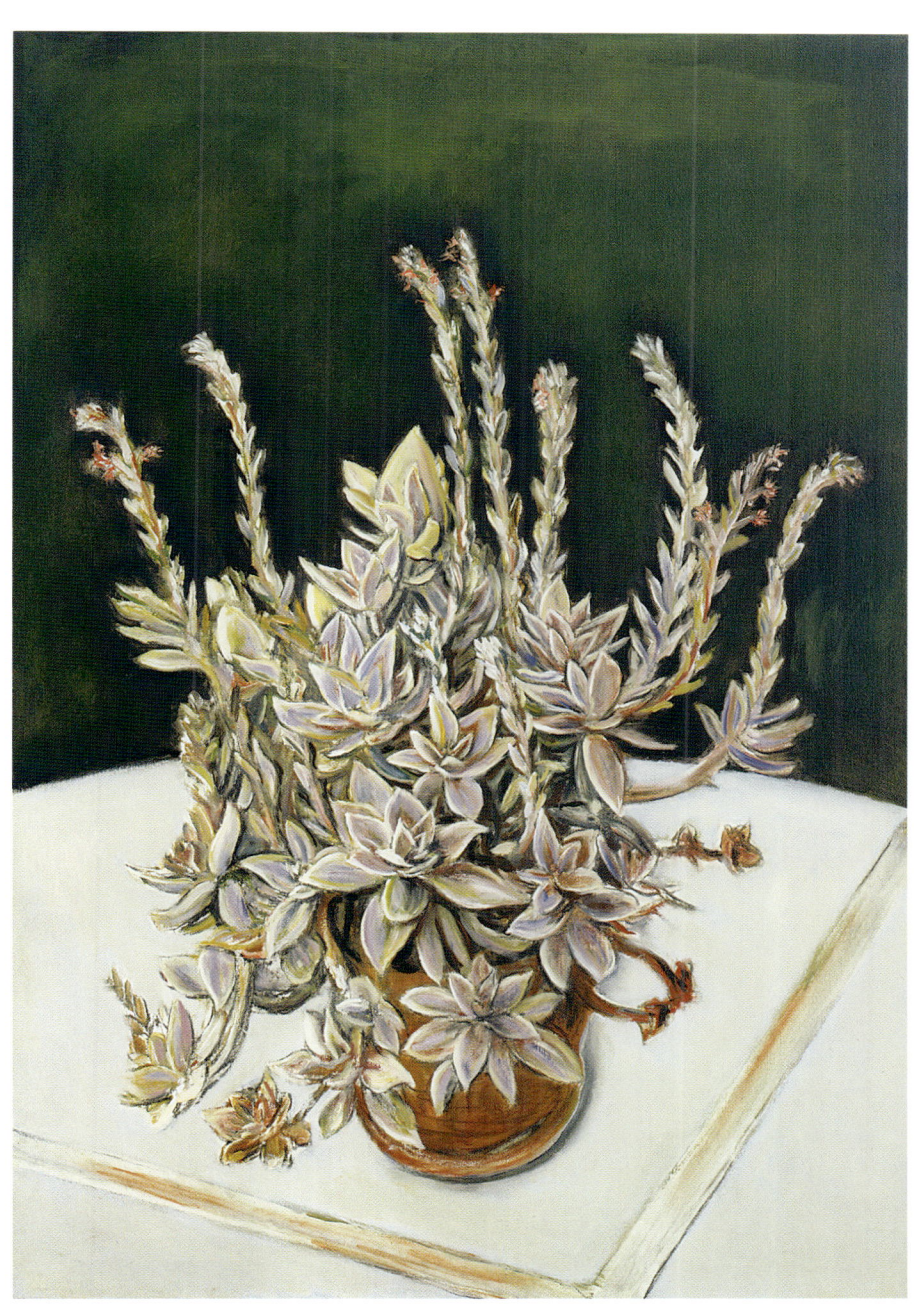

3 graptopetalum

december 1975

oil on canvas

48 x 33 inches

121.9 x 83.8 centimeters

4 san gorgonio

may 1976

oil on canvas

49 x 54 inches

124.5 x 137.2 centimeters

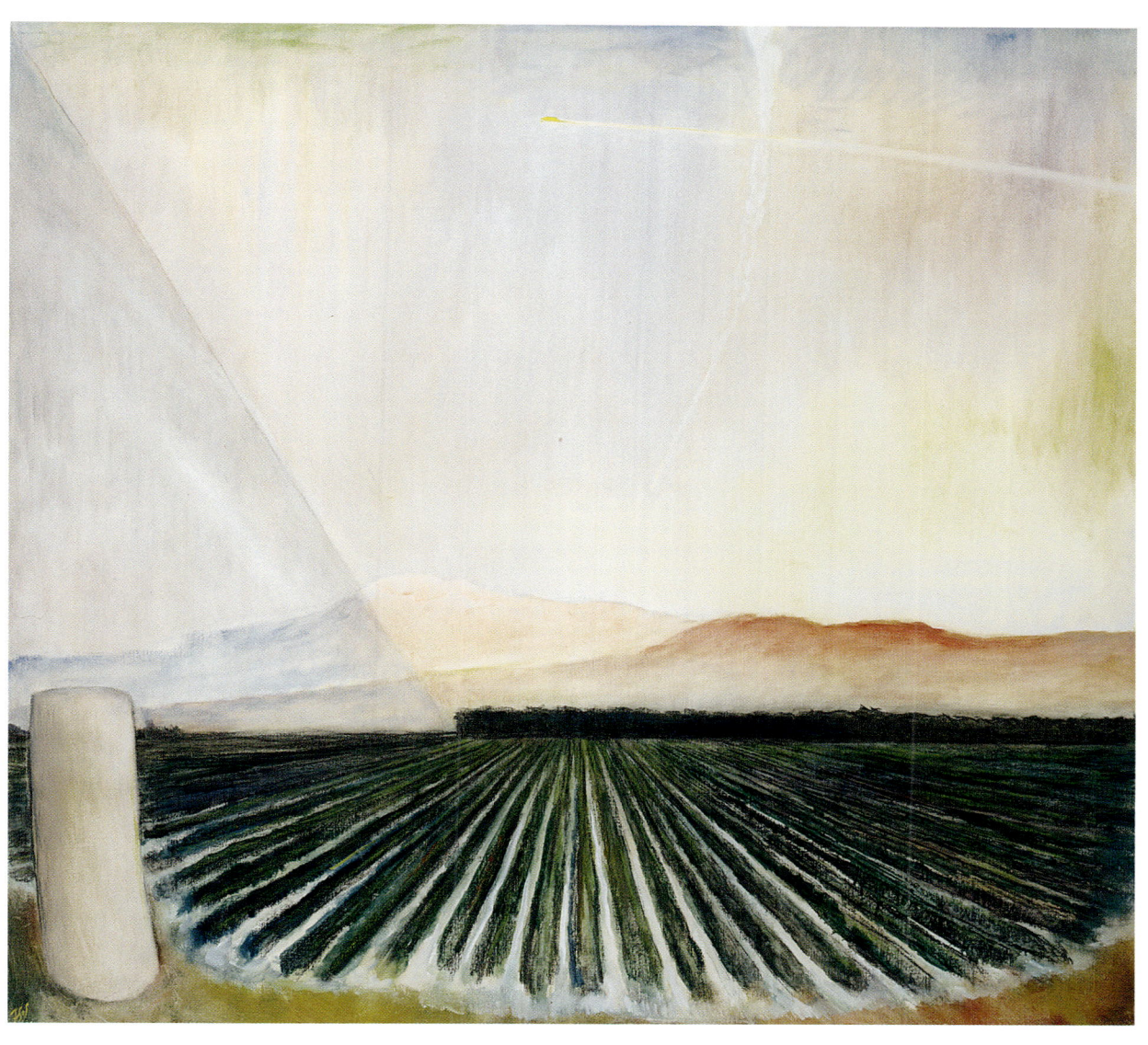

5 two palms, evening II

april 1977

oil on canvas

38 x 49 inches

96.5 x 124.5 centimeters

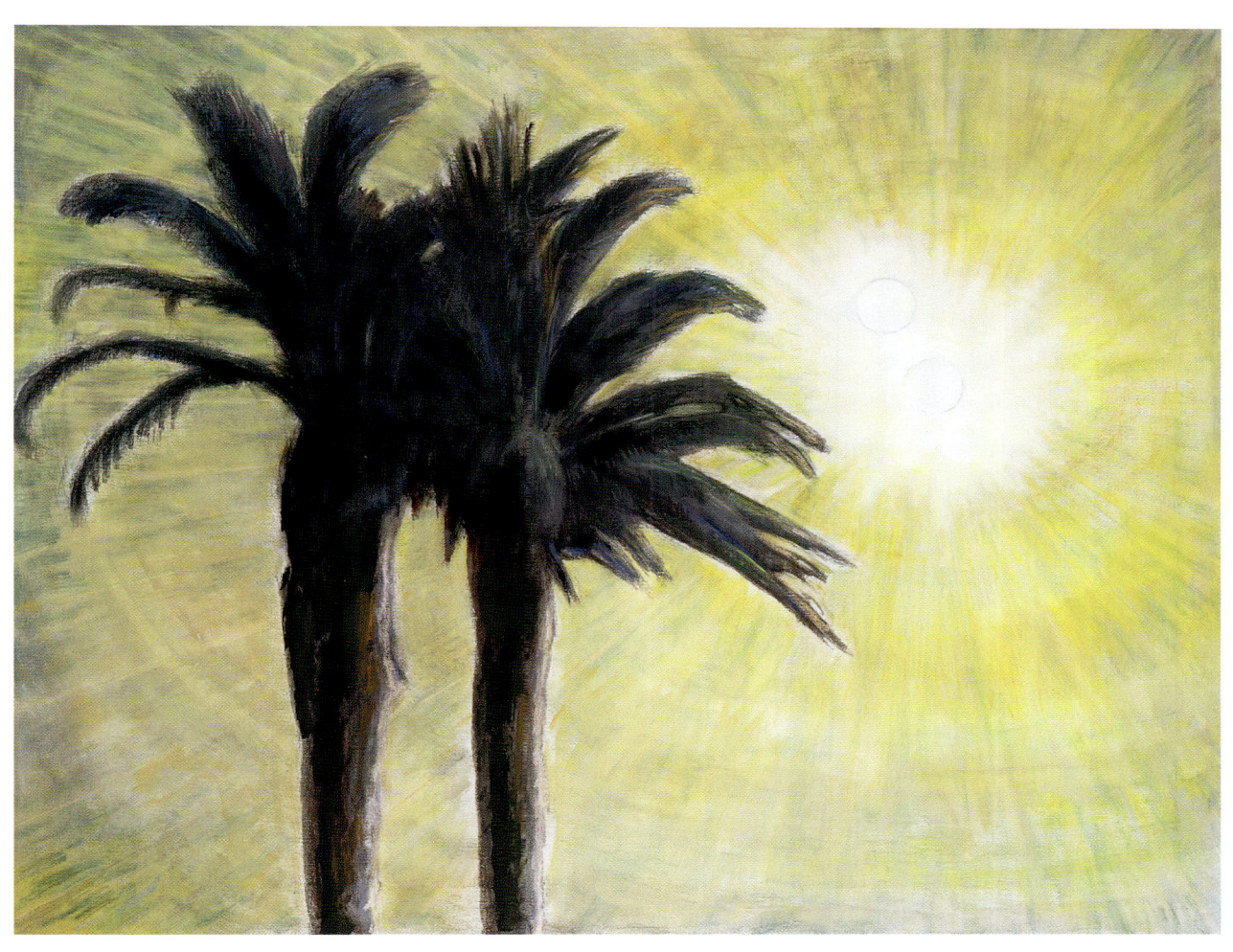

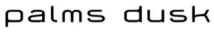

palms dusk

january 1978

oil on canvas

59 x 52 inches

149.9 x 132.1 centimeters

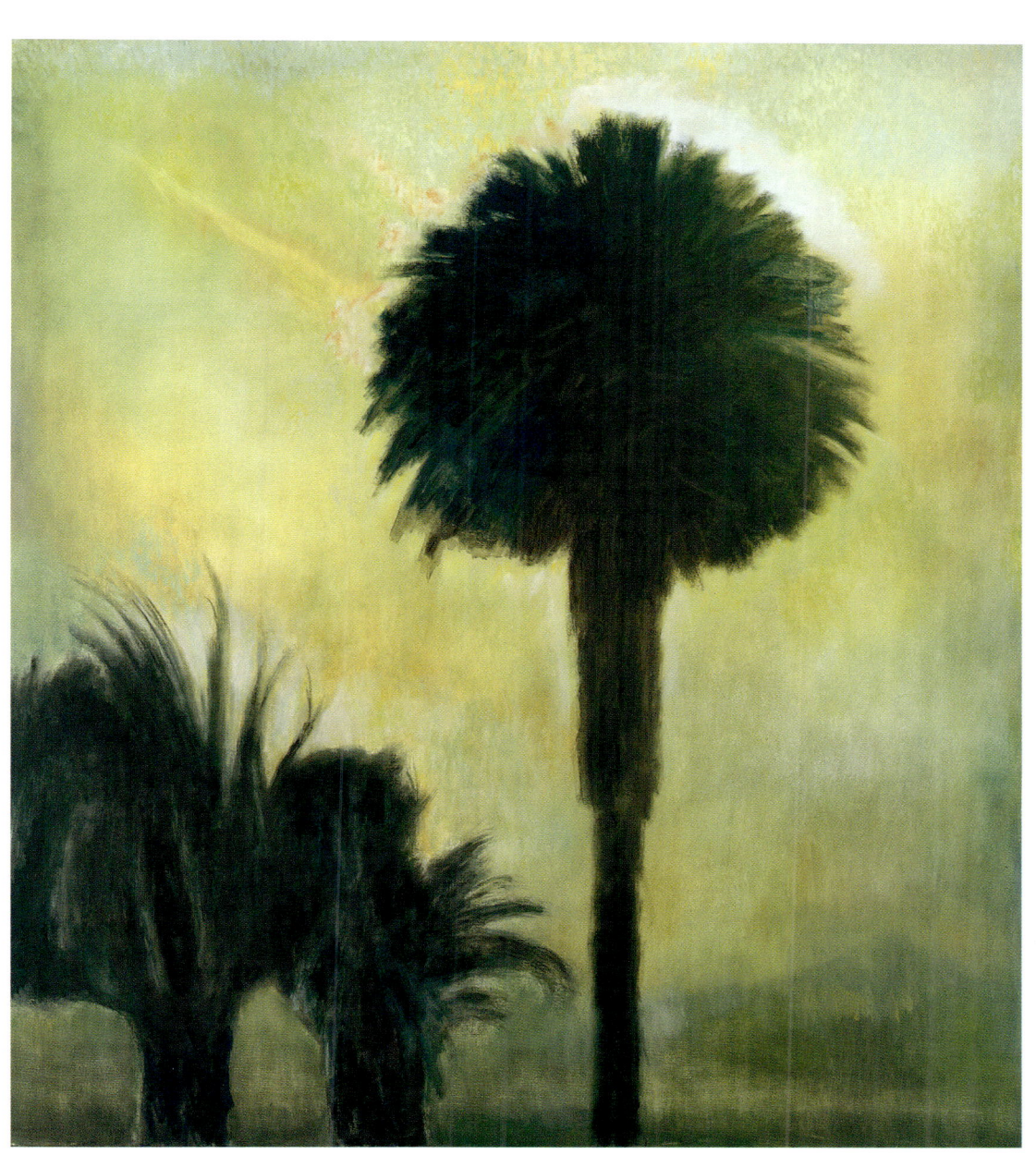

7 the garden

may 1978

oil on canvas

96 x 48 inches

243.9 x 121.9 centimeters

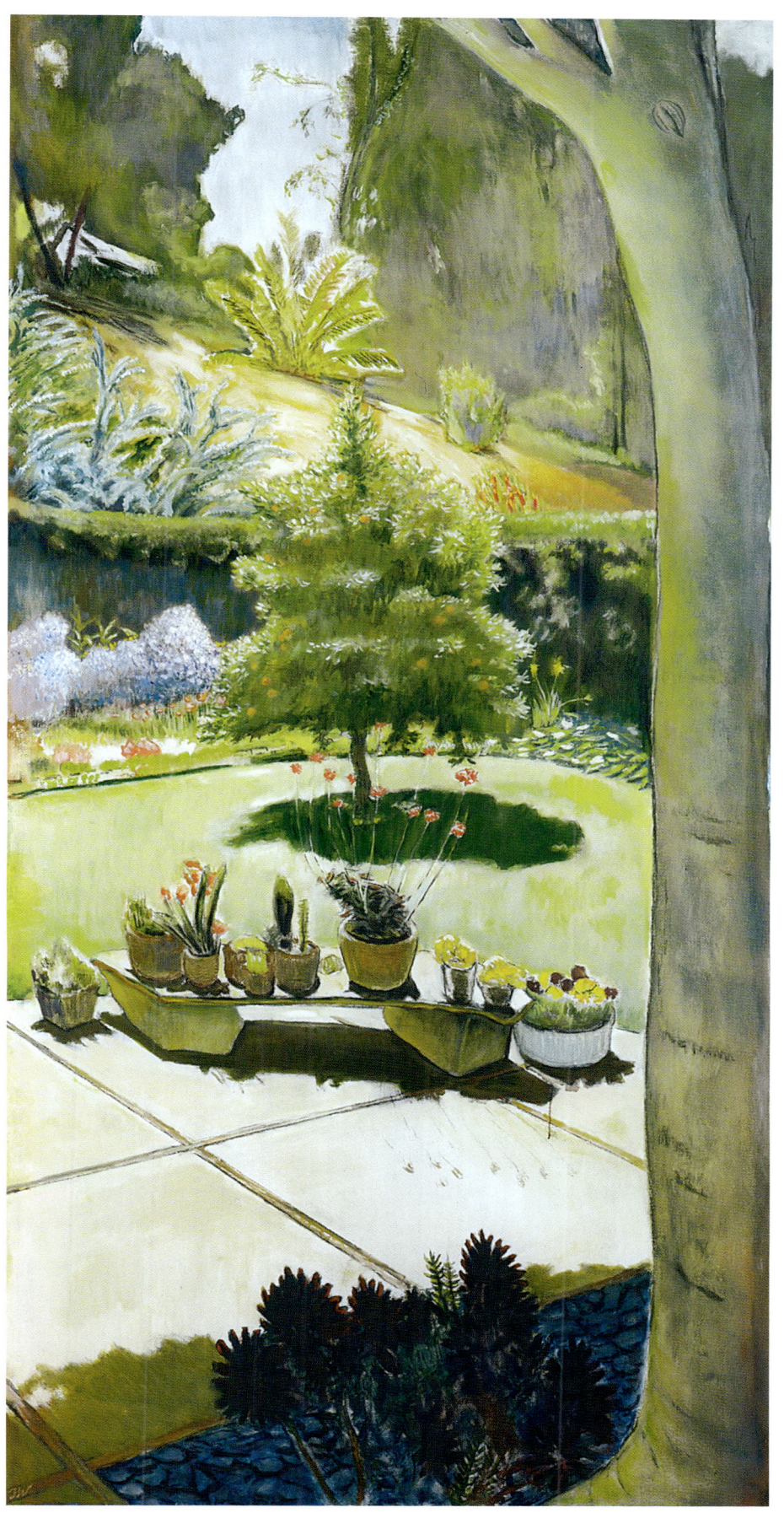

8 the new tree

january 1979

oil on canvas

96 x 51 inches

243.9 x 129.5 centimeters

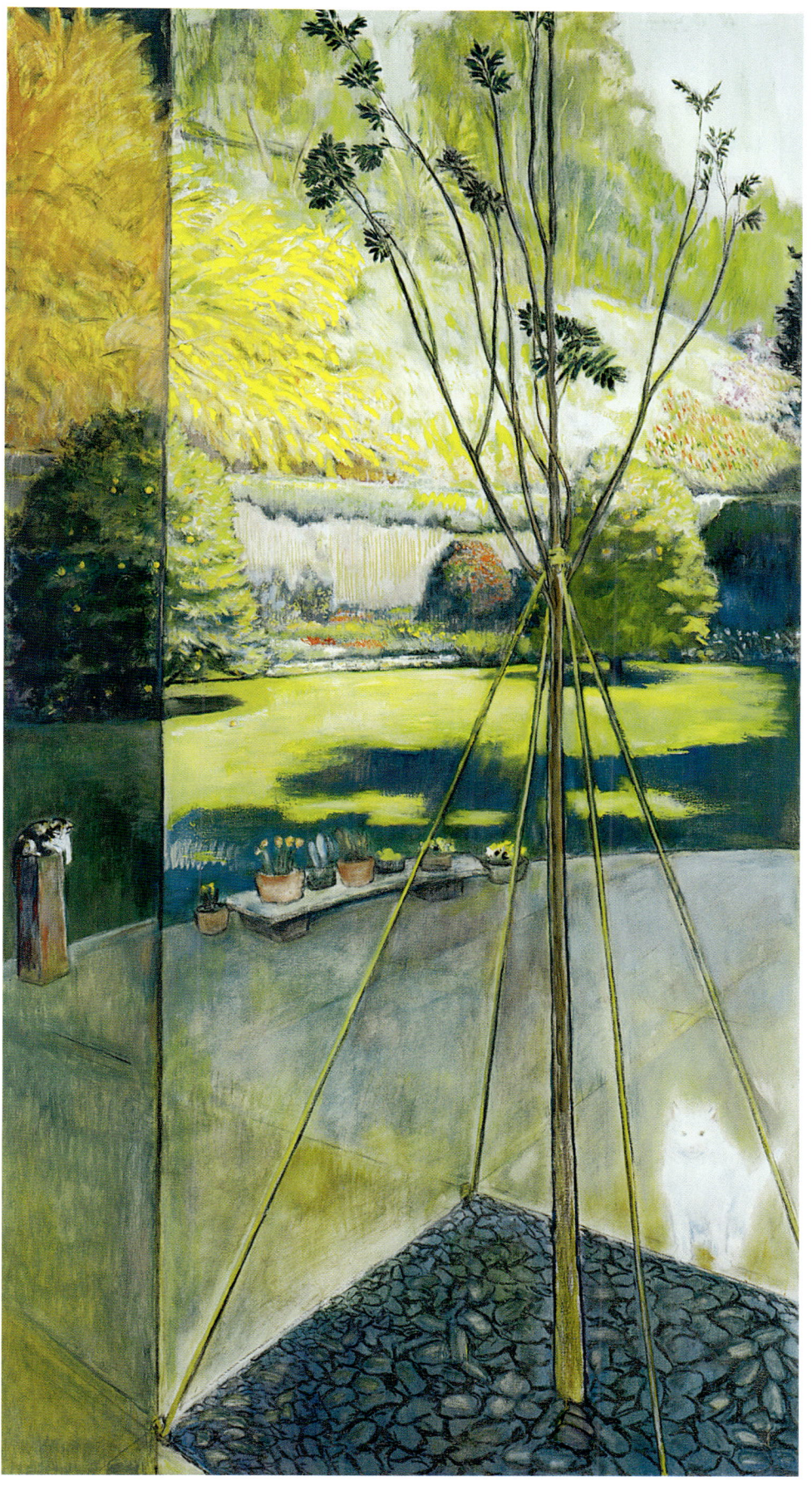

9 monte rosa and three palms

january 1979

oil on canvas

51 x 59 inches

129.5 x 149.9 centimeters

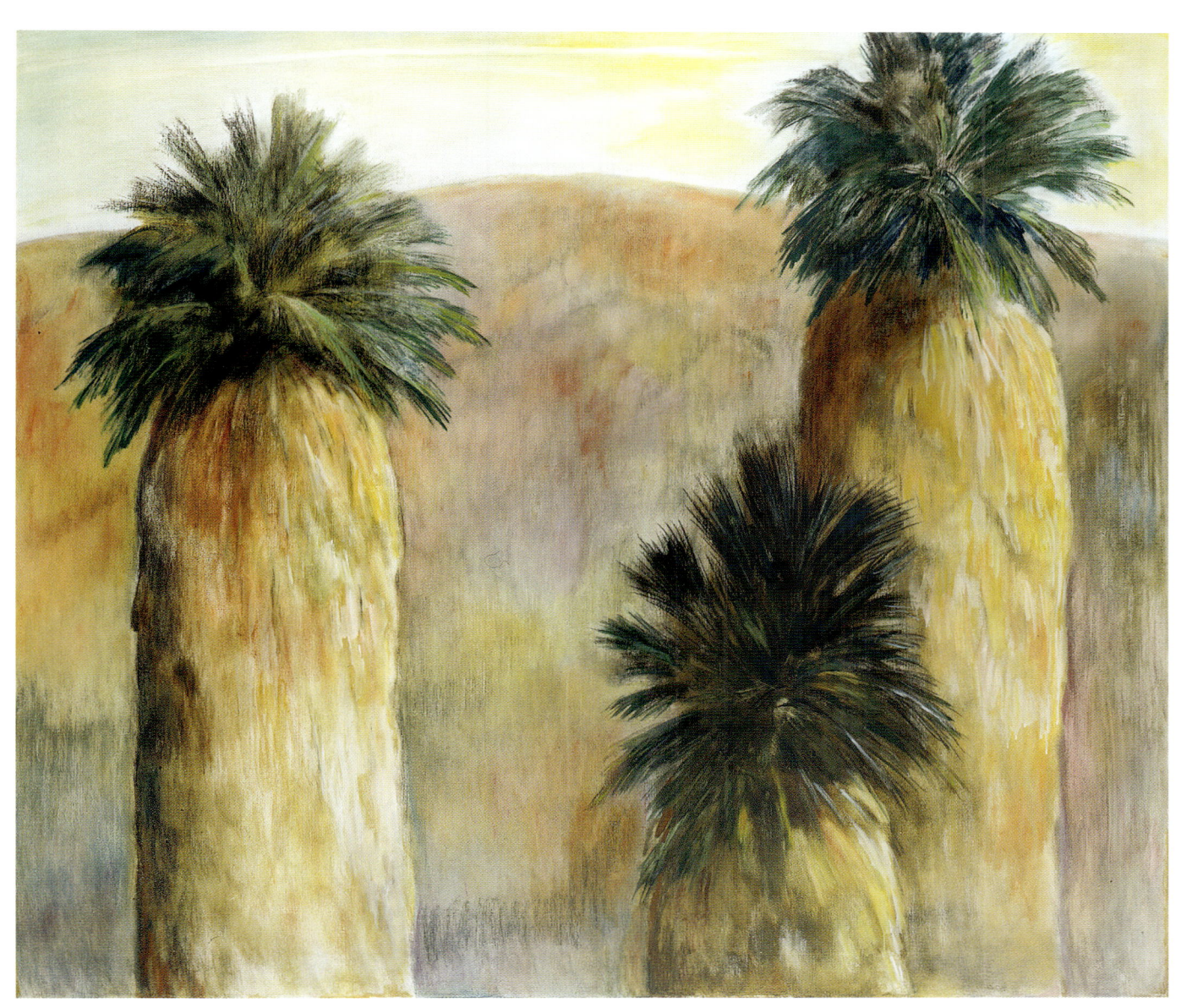

10 short night

february 1979

oil on canvas

40 x 99 inches

101.6 x 251.5 centimeters

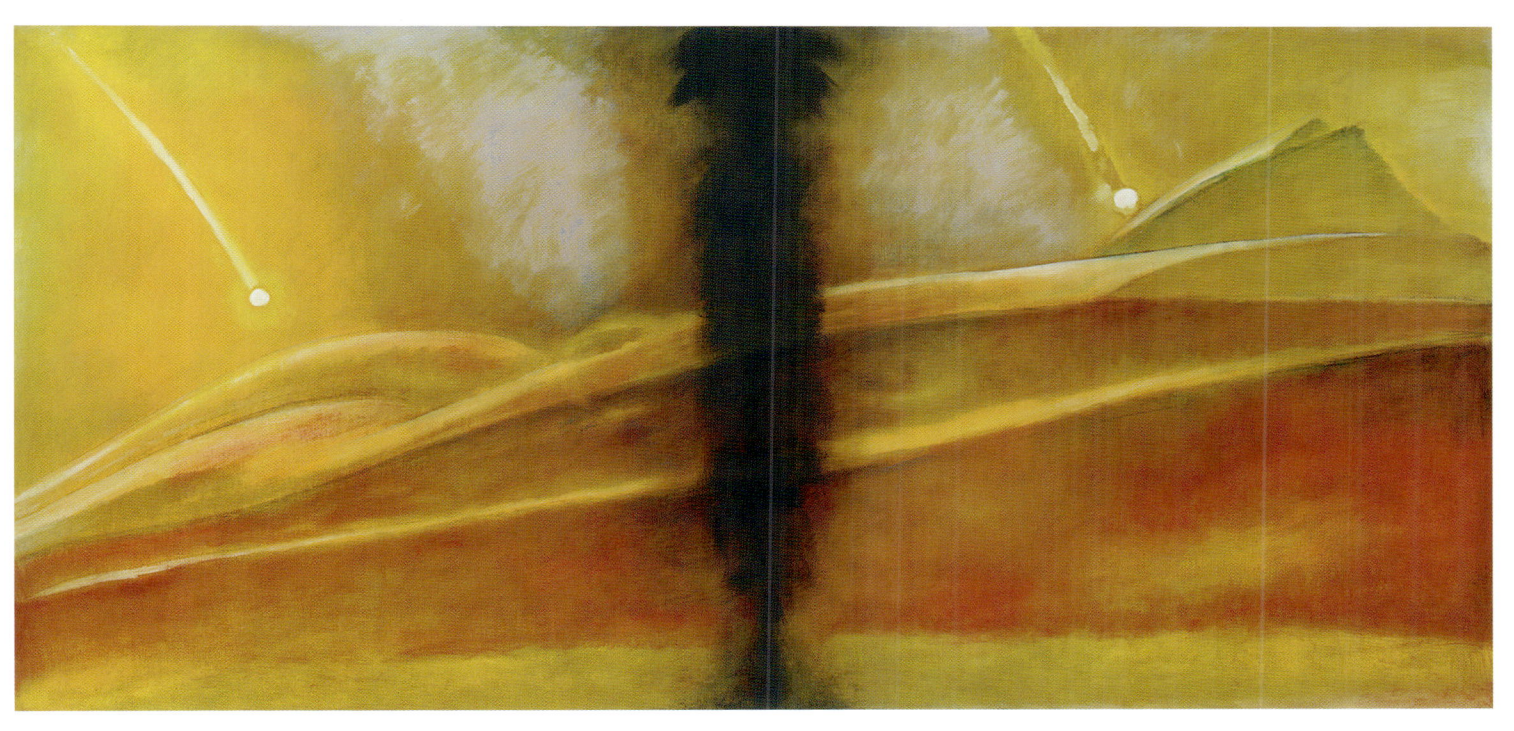

11 morning hours

june 1979

oil on canvas

72 x 50 inches

182.9 x 127 centimeters

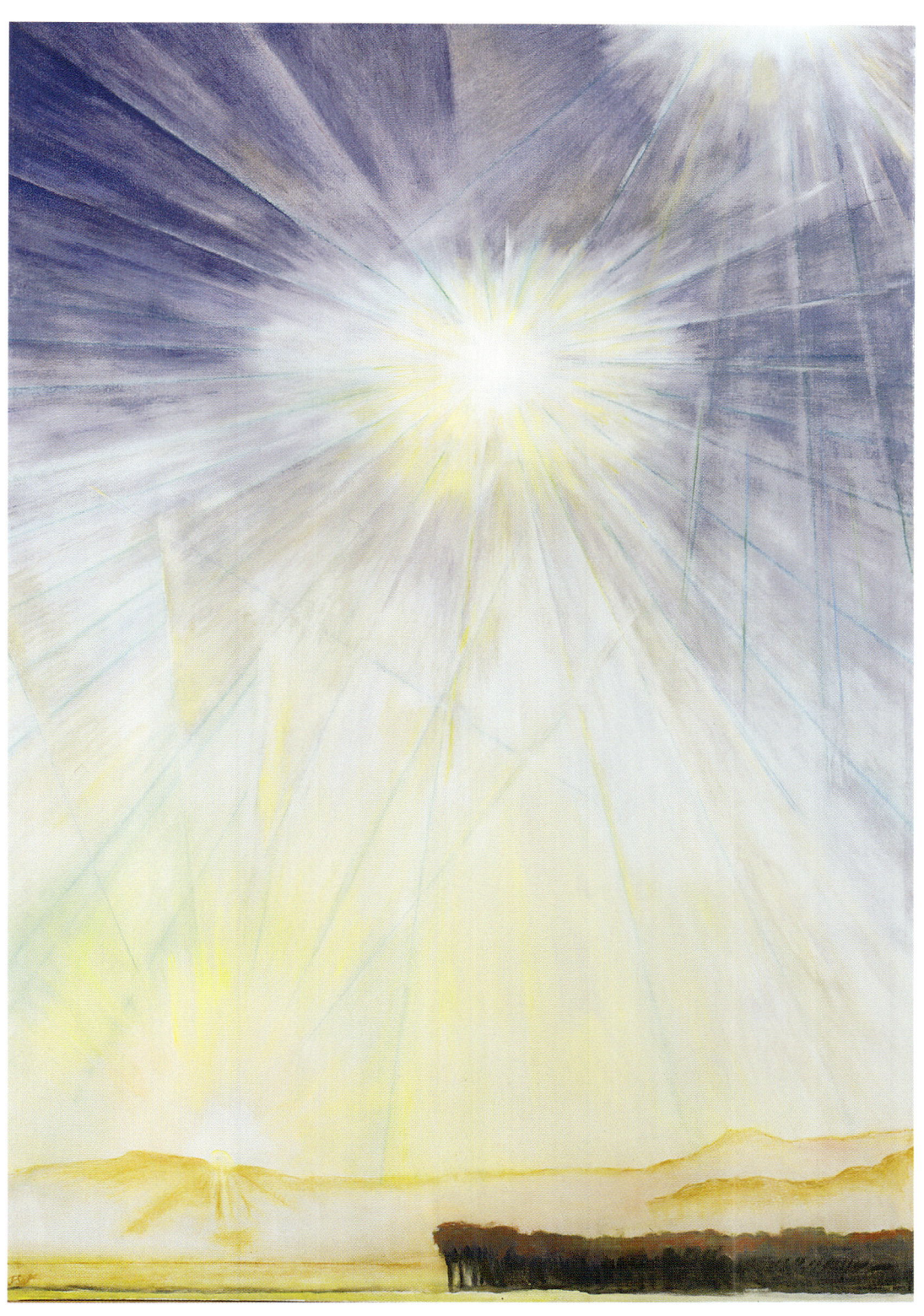

12 **suddenly afternoon**

july 1979

oil on canvas

98 x 70 inches

248.9 x 177.8 centimeters

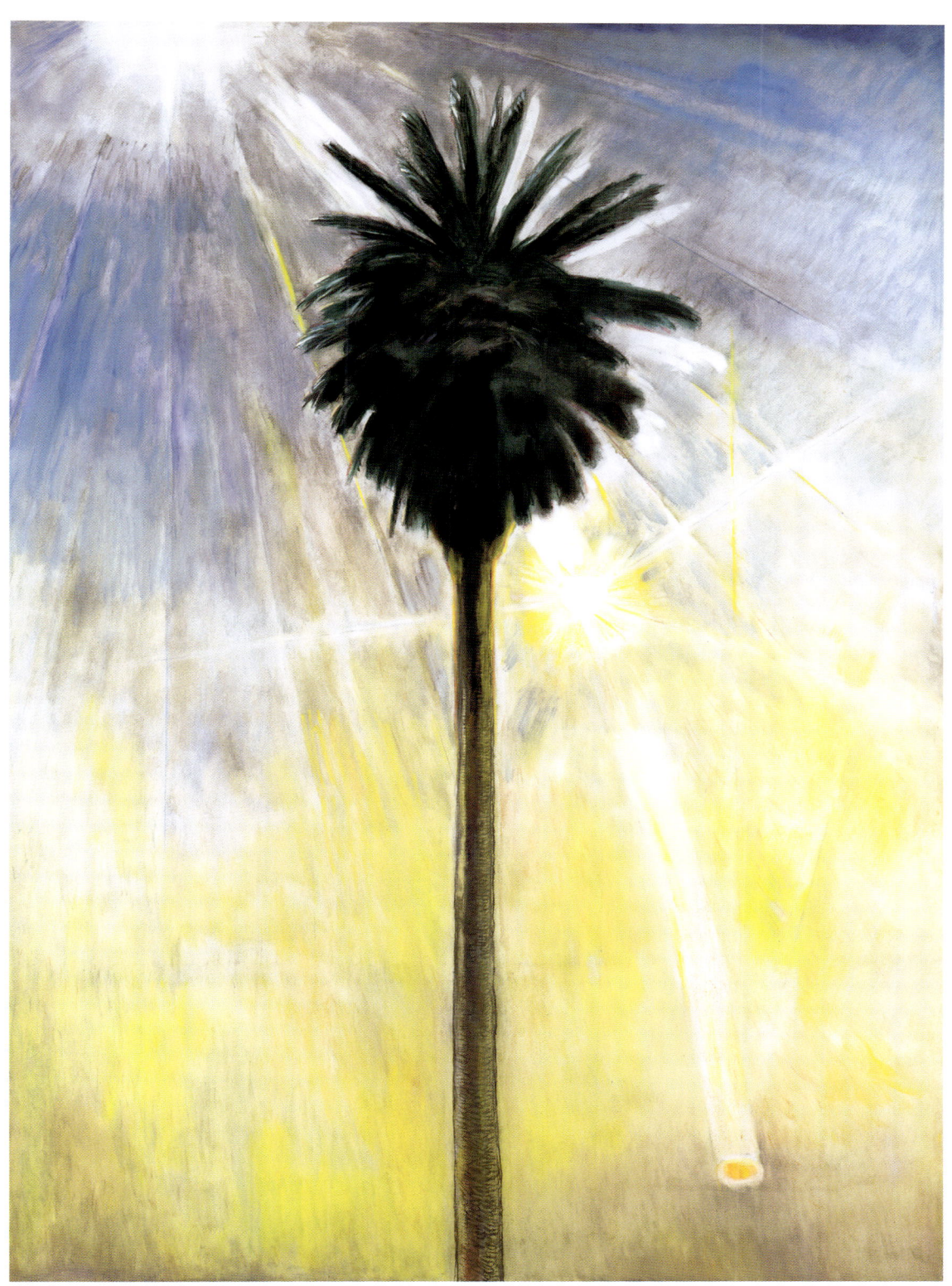

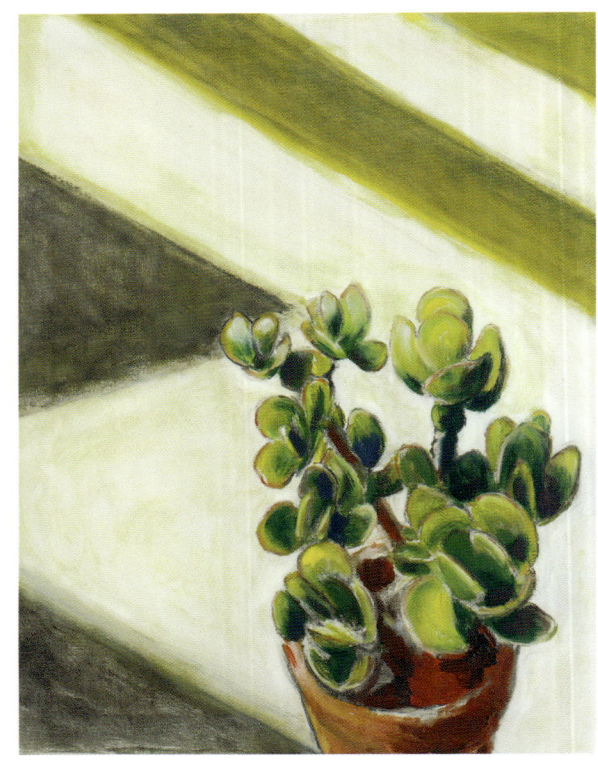

13 succulent

april 1980

oil on canvas

29 x 22 inches

73.7 x 55.9 centimeters

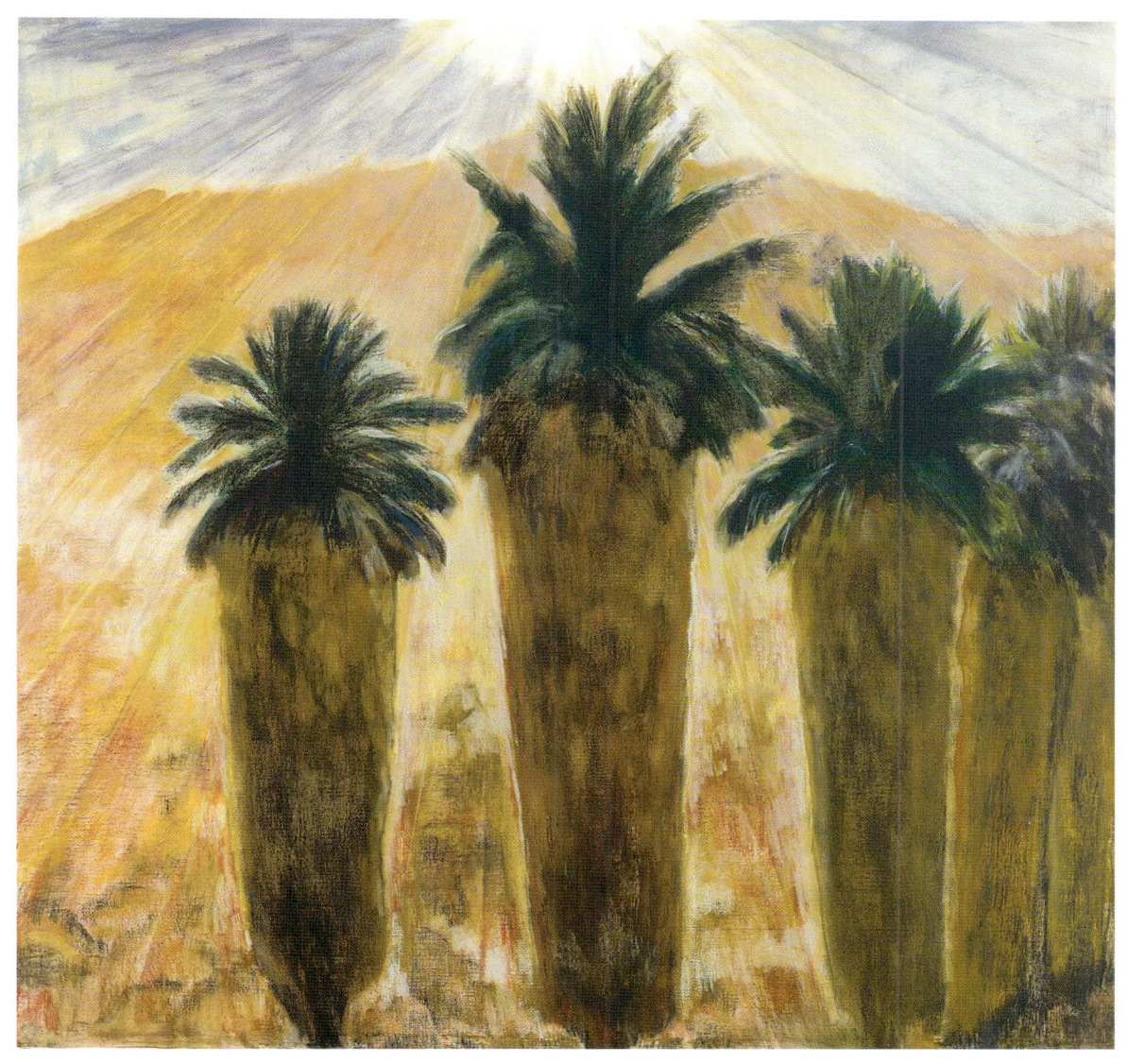

four palms and a mountain (monte rosa)

may 1980

oil on canvas

47 x 48 inches

119.4 x 121.9 centimeters

15 entrance to the ranch

august 1980

oil on canvas

51 x 73 inches

129.5 x 185.4 centimeters

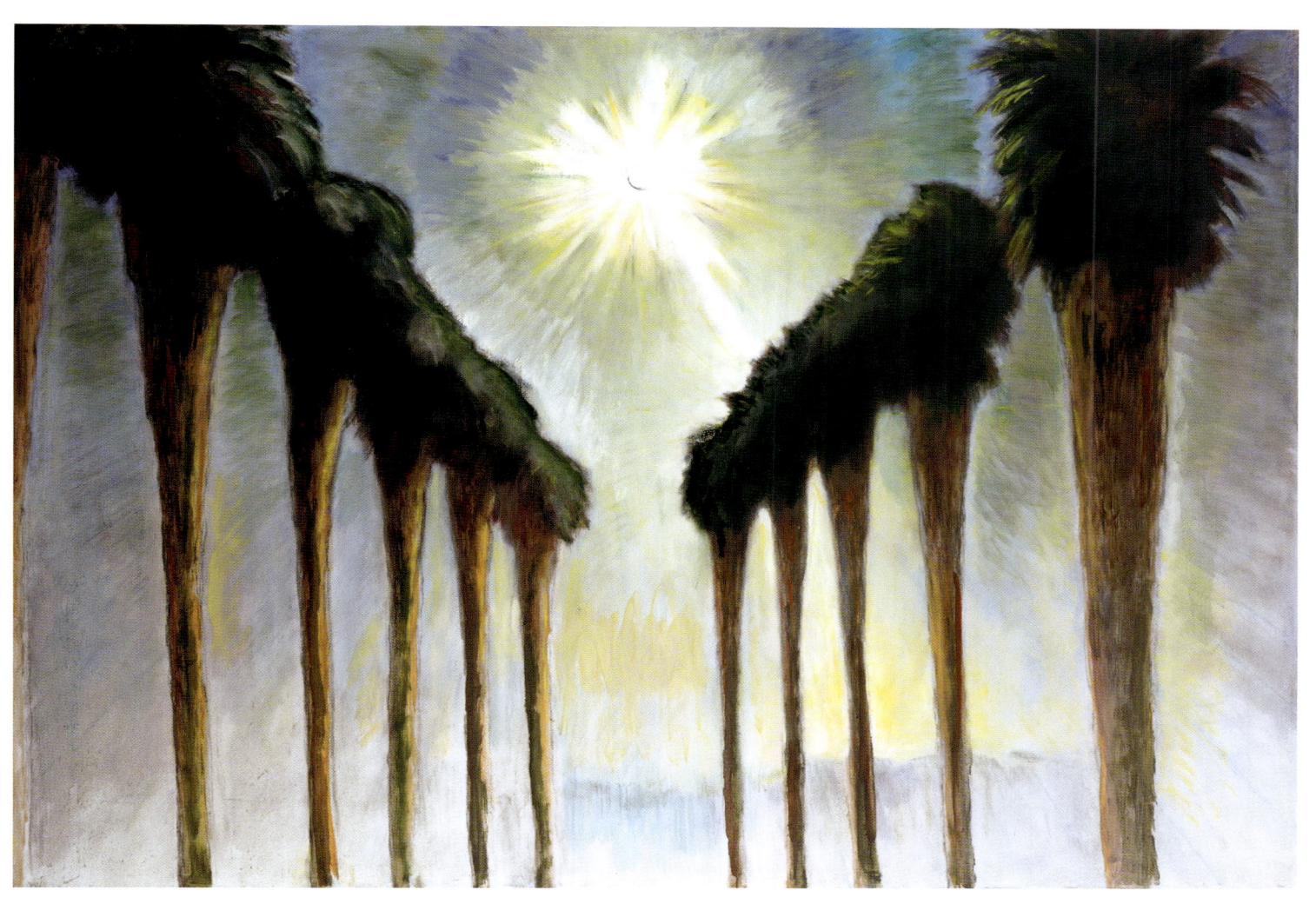

16 blue islands

december 1980

oil on canvas

50 x 72 inches

127 x 182.9 centimeters

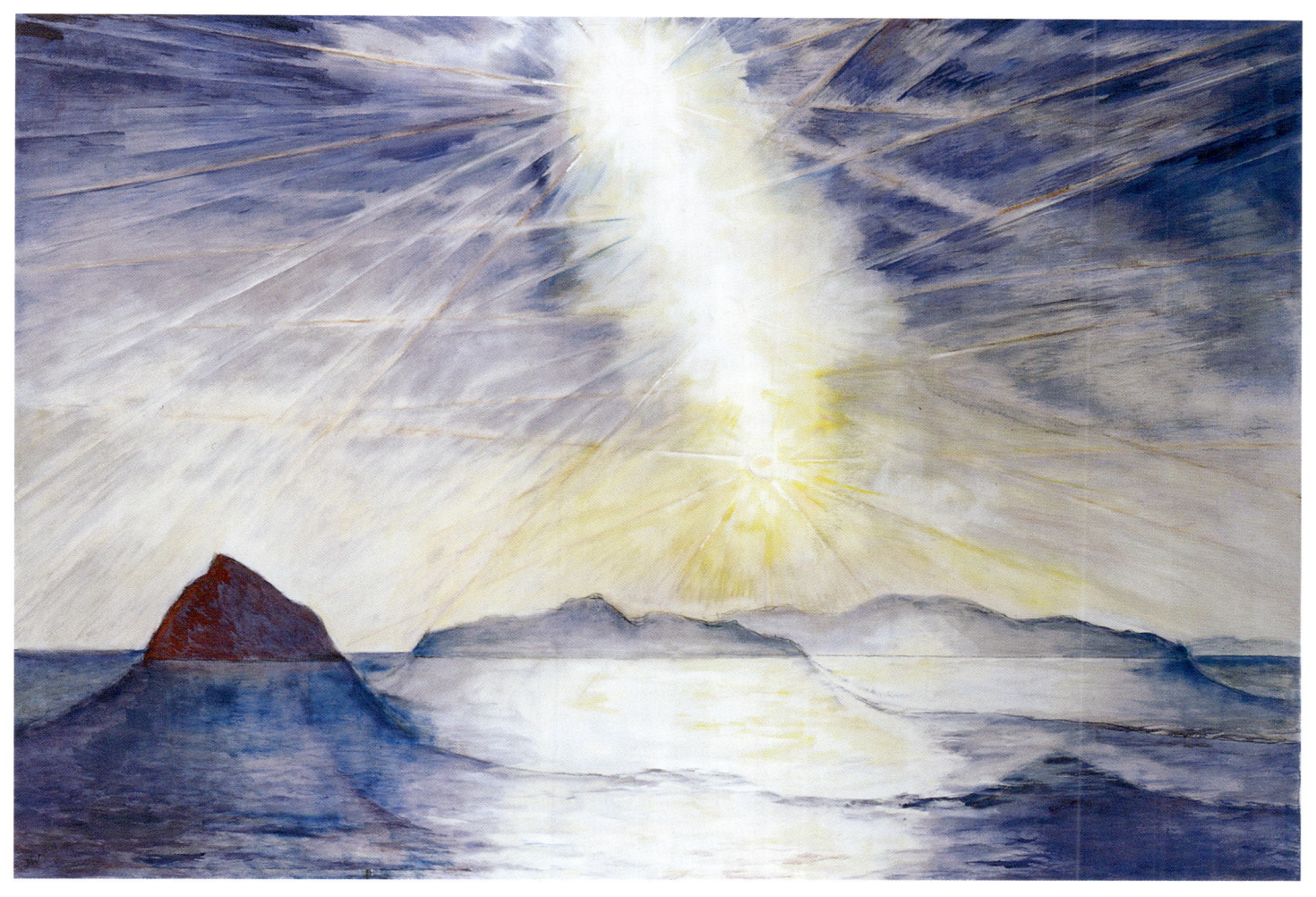

17 desert morning
(morning hours II)

january 1981

oil on canvas

78 x 50 inches

198.1 x 127 centimeters

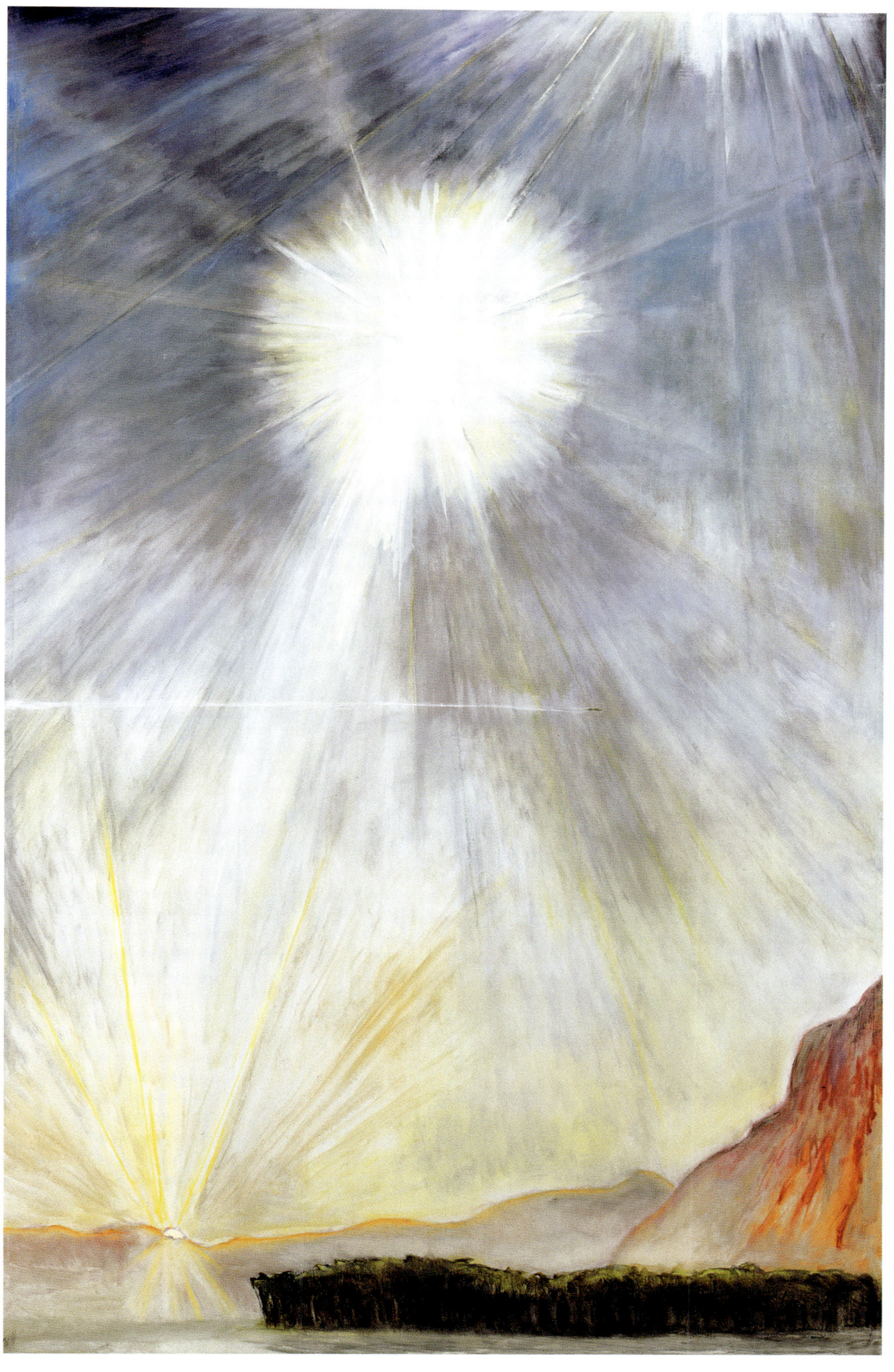

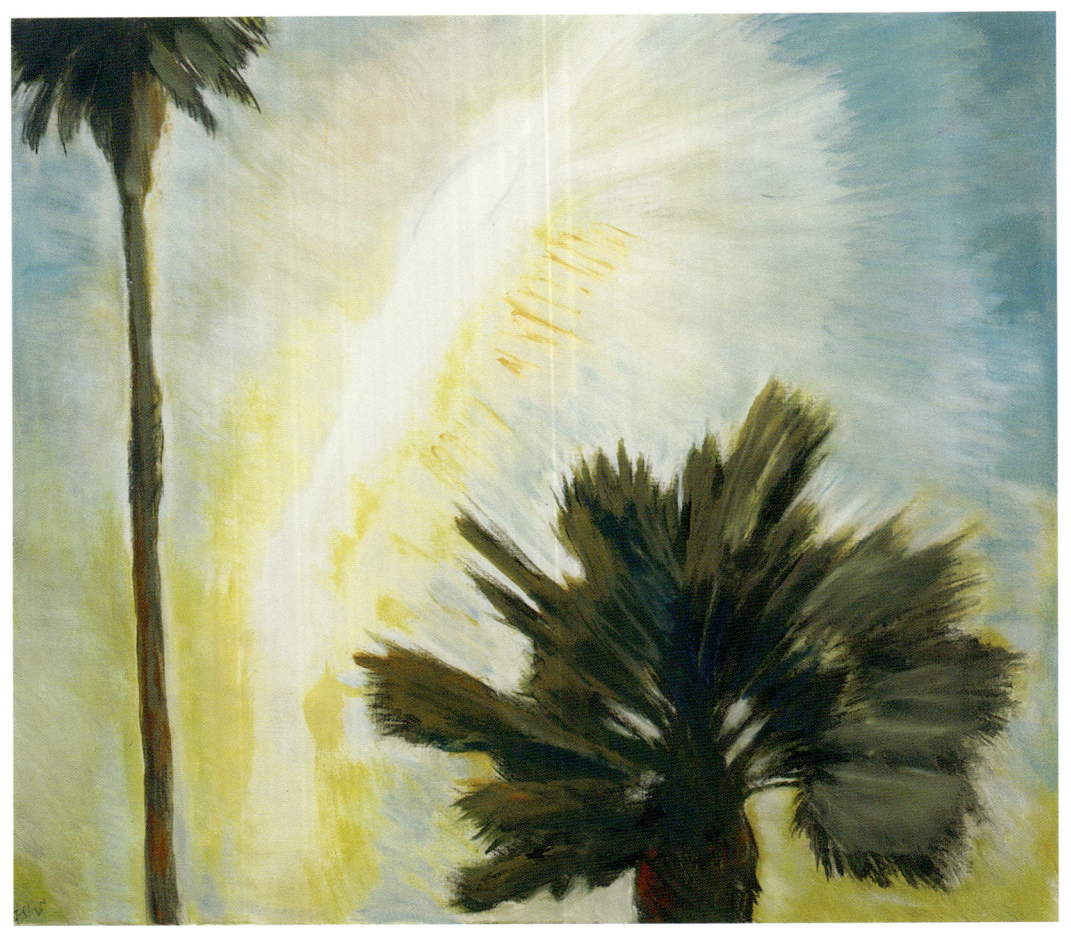

18 tame palms

march 1982

oil on canvas

36 x 40 inches

91.4 x 101.6 centimeters

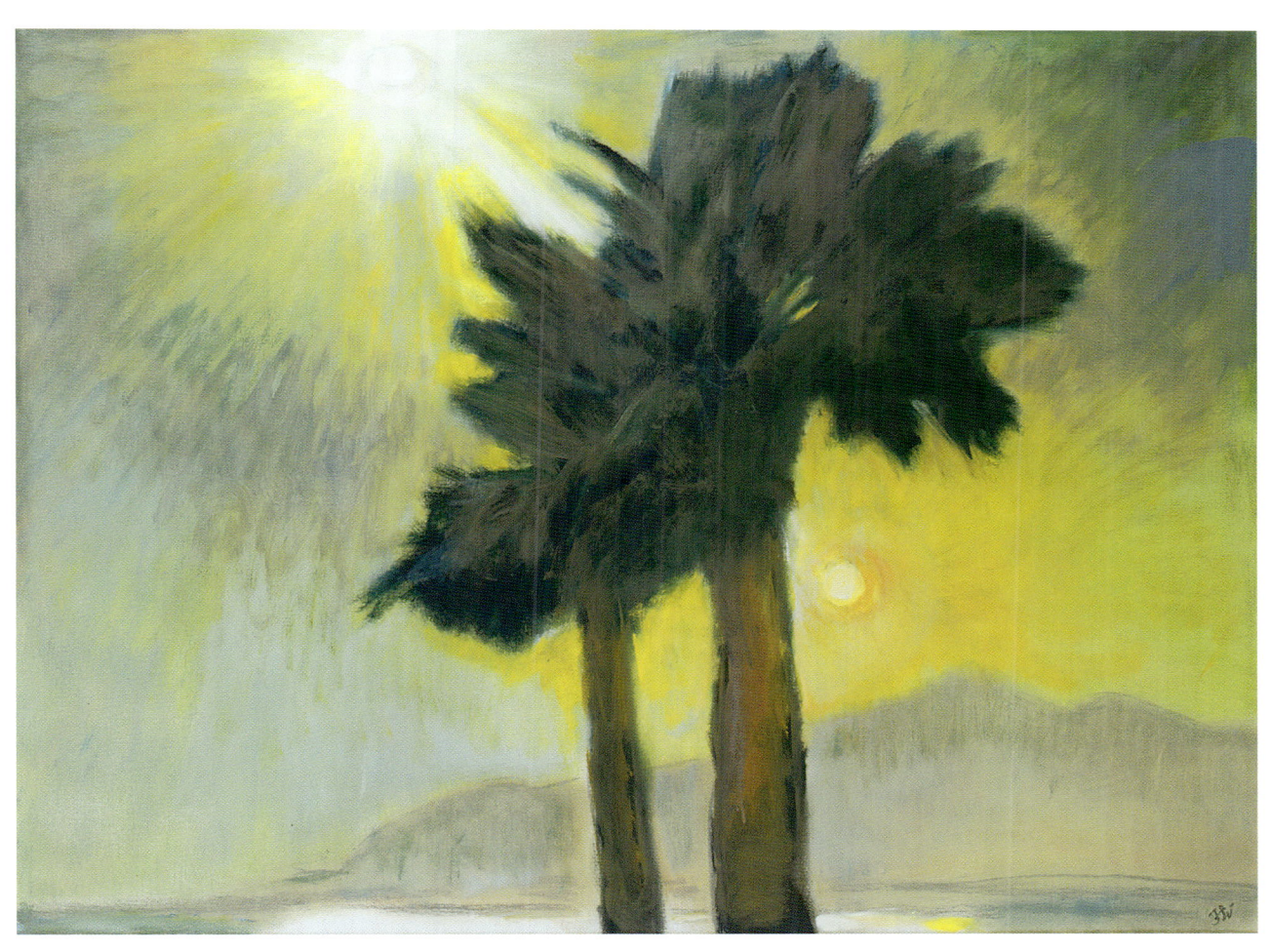

looking west

august 1982

oil on canvas

36 x 48 inches

91.4 x 121.9 centimeters

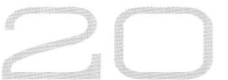

returning day

august 1982

oil on canvas

48 x 66 inches

121.9 x 167.6 centimeters

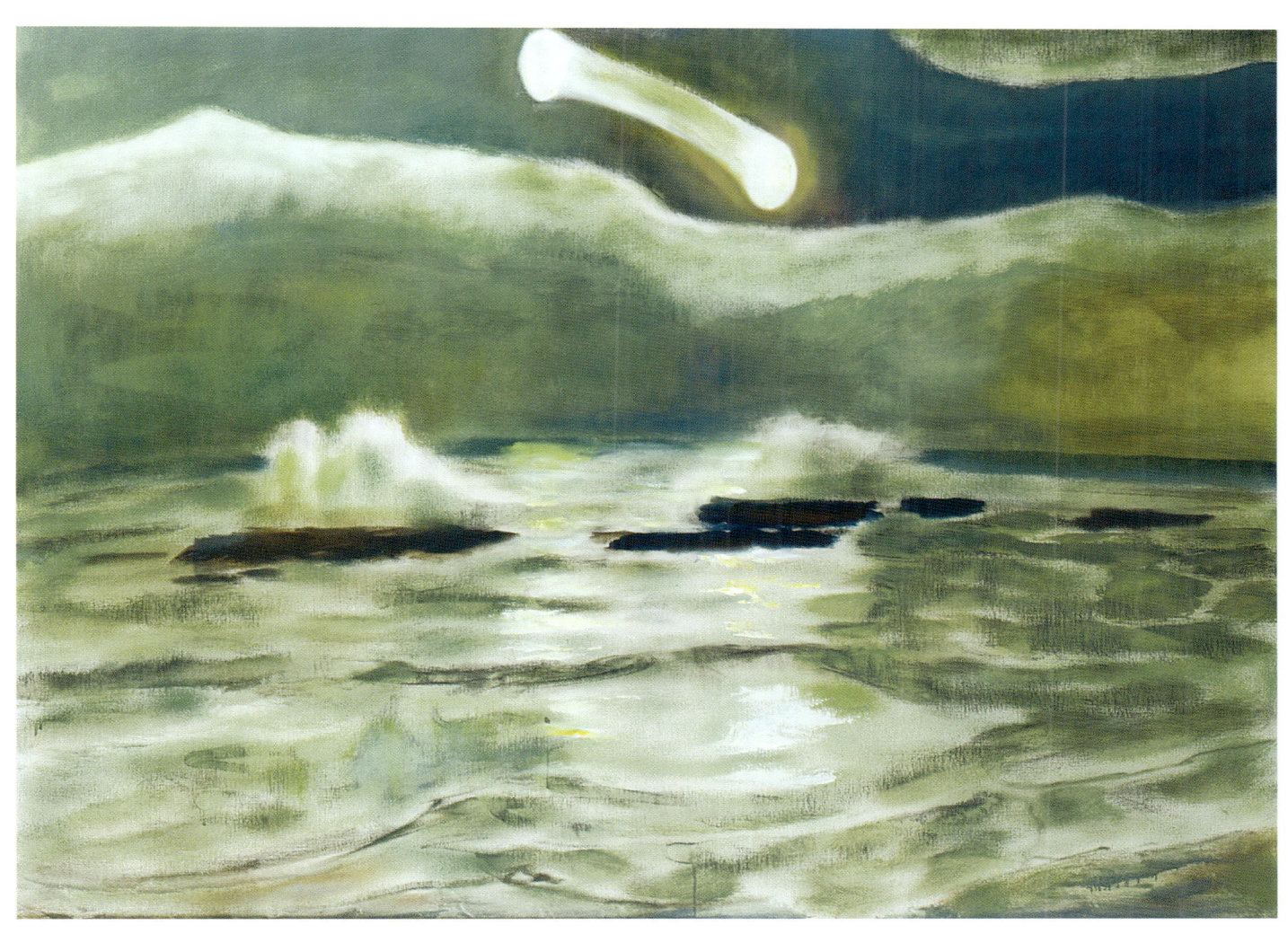

21   **santa ana blowing** (diptych)

october 1982

oil on canvas

96 x 36 inches

243.8 x 91.4 centimeters

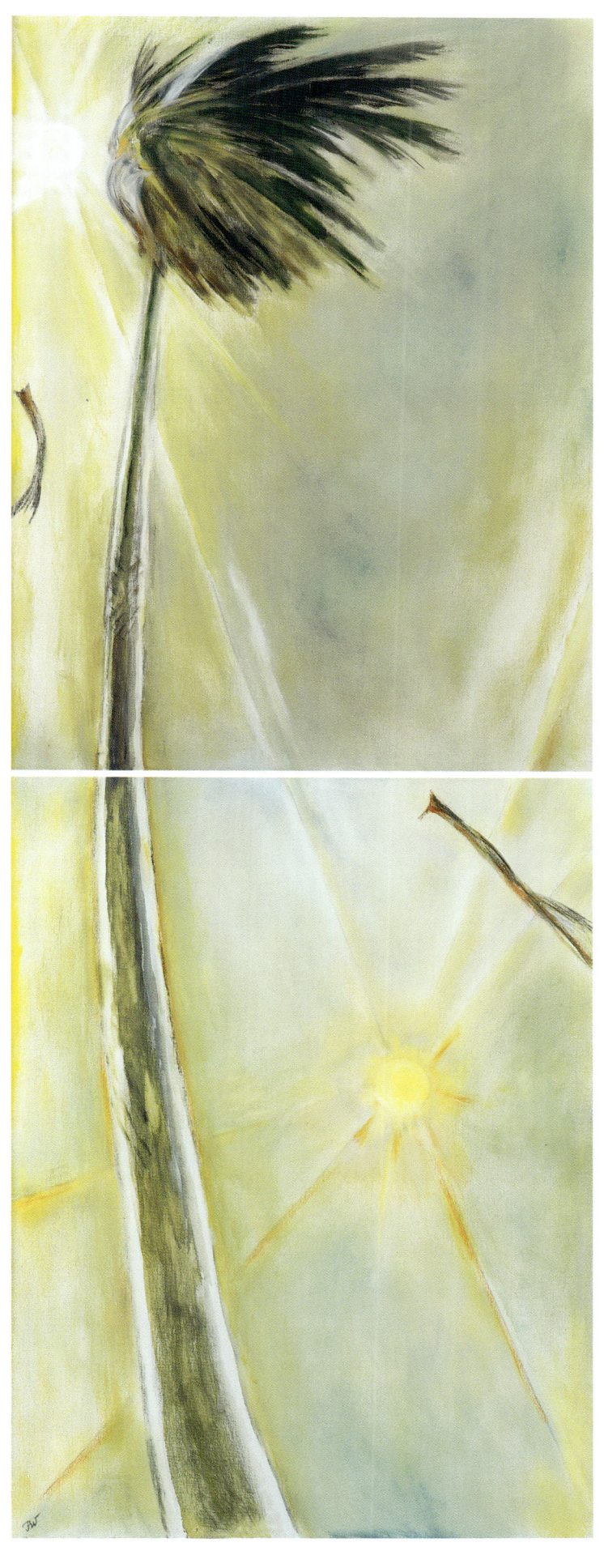

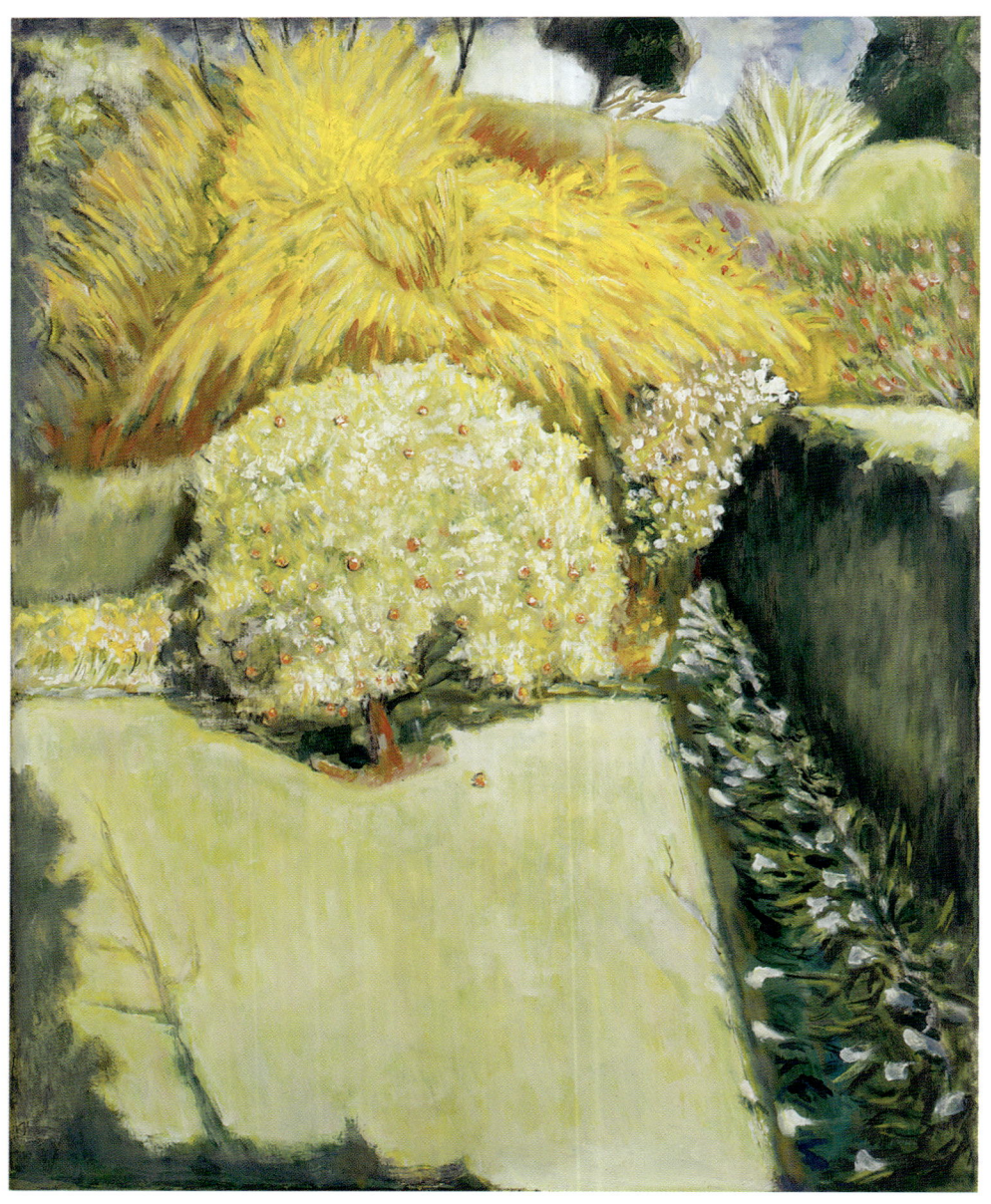

22 midwinter

april 1983

oil on canvas

50 x 40 inches

127 x 101.6 centimeters

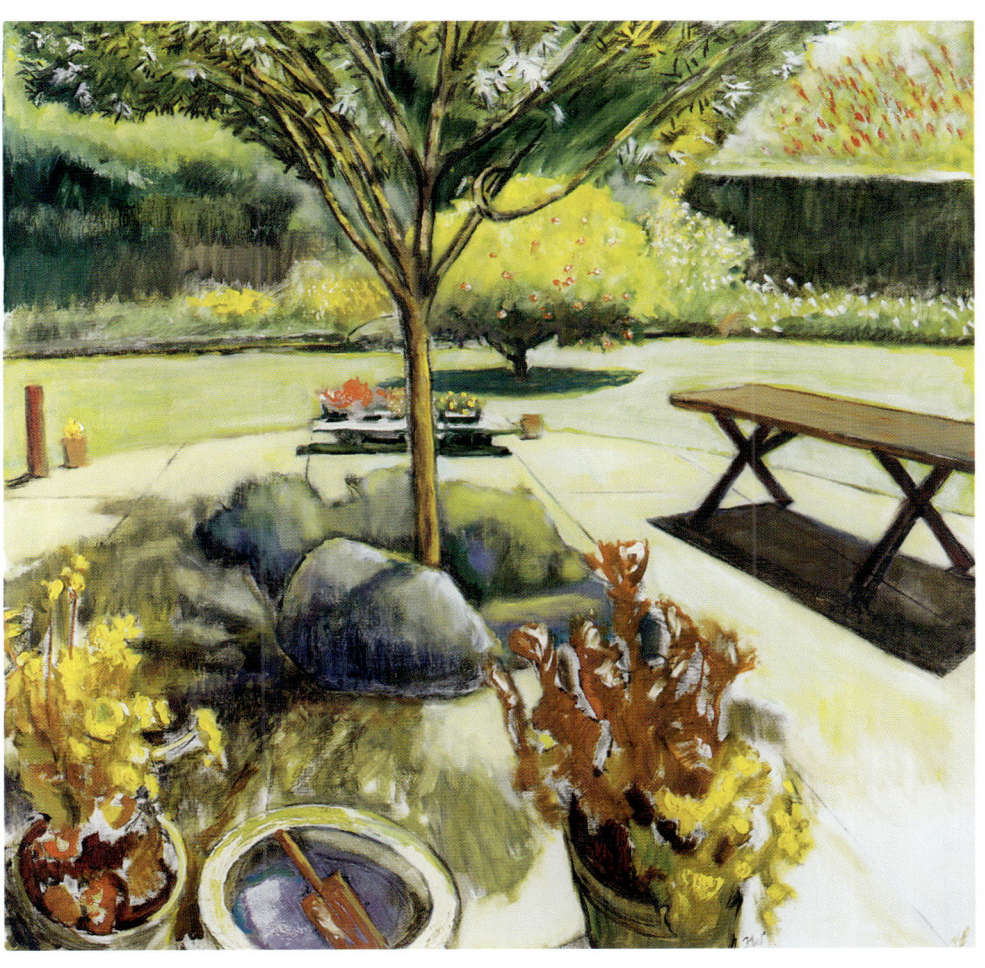

23 midwinter II

april 1983

oil on canvas

48 x 48 inches

121.9 x 121.9 centimeters

24 spring

may 1983

oil on canvas

48 x 48 inches

121.9 x 121.9 centimeters

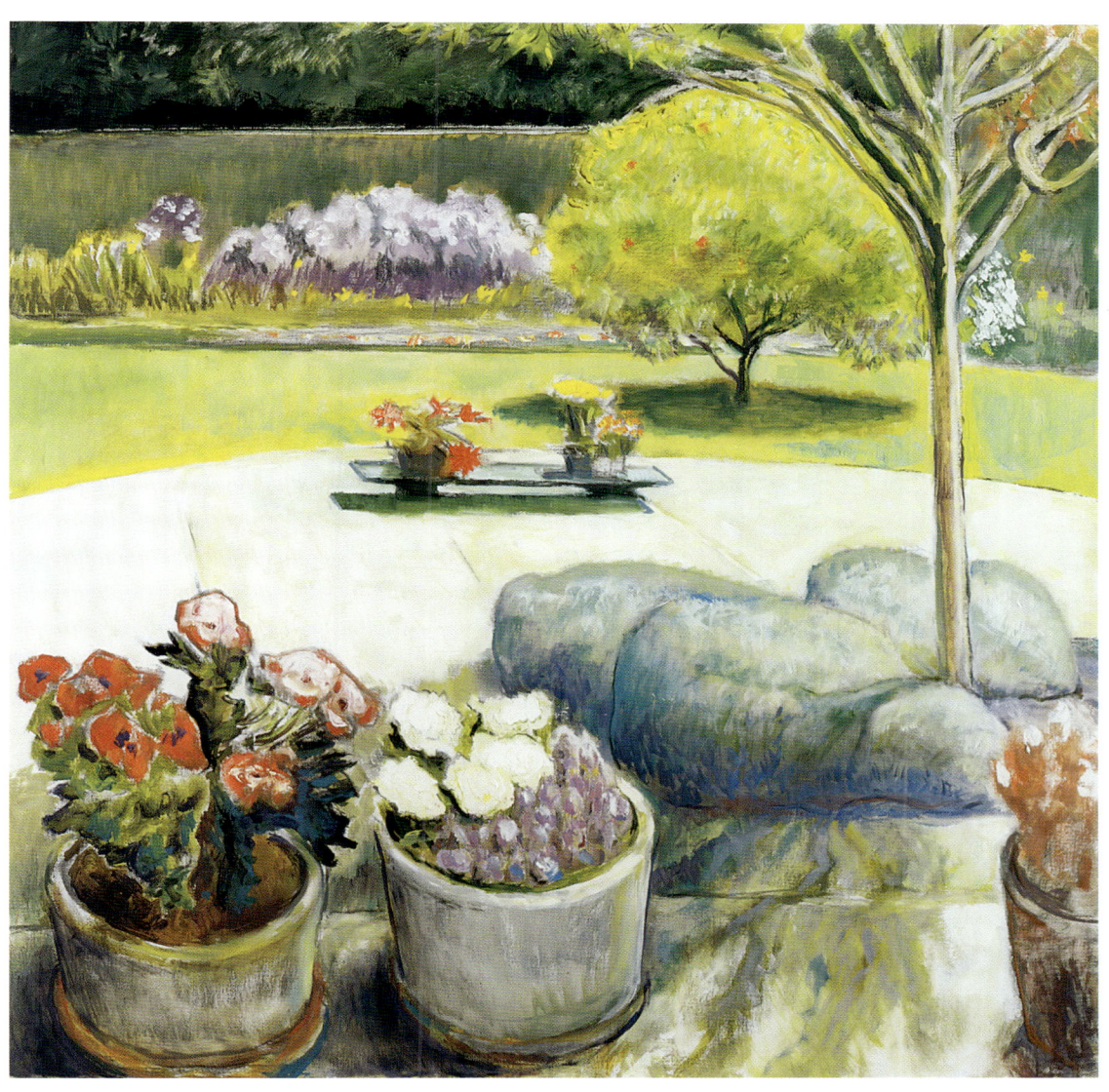

25 pacific

may 1983

oil on canvas

48 x 66 inches

121.9 x 167.6 centimeters

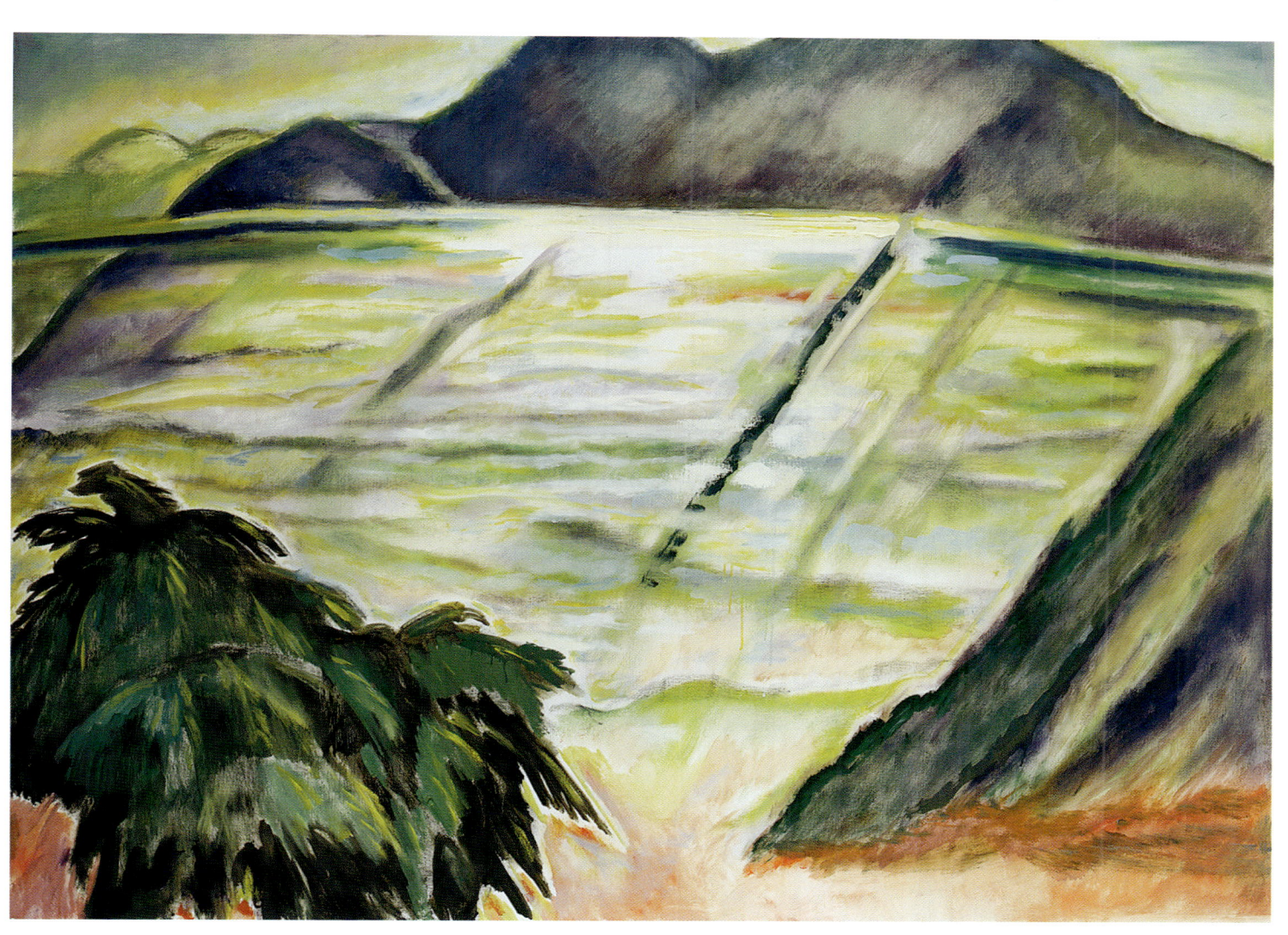

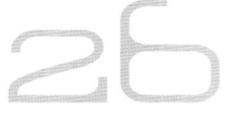 six palms

june 1983

oil on canvas

40 x 46 inches

101.6 x 116.8 centimeters

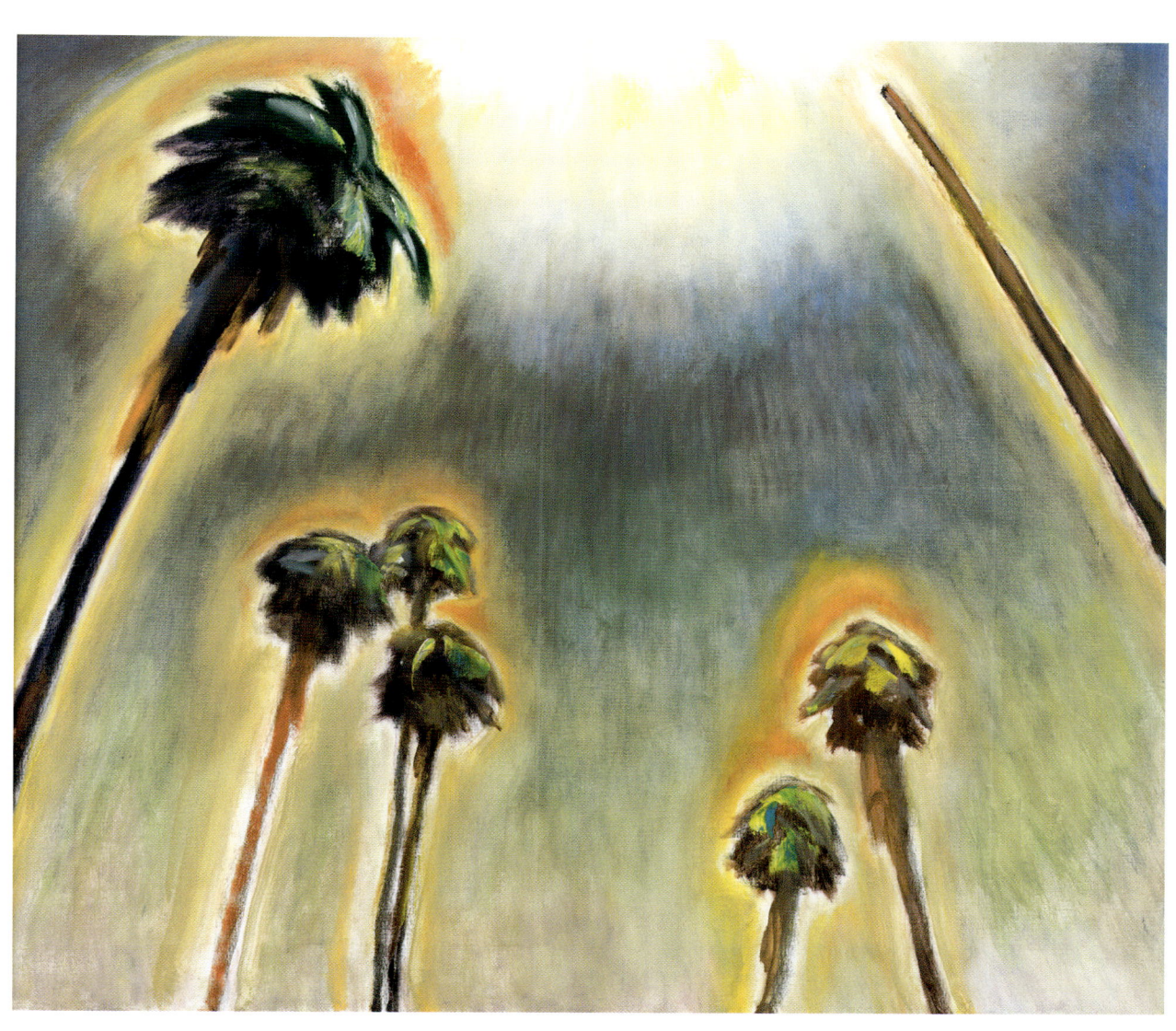

27 orchid cactus II

july 1983

oil on canvas

44 x 44 inches

111.8 x 111.8 centimeters

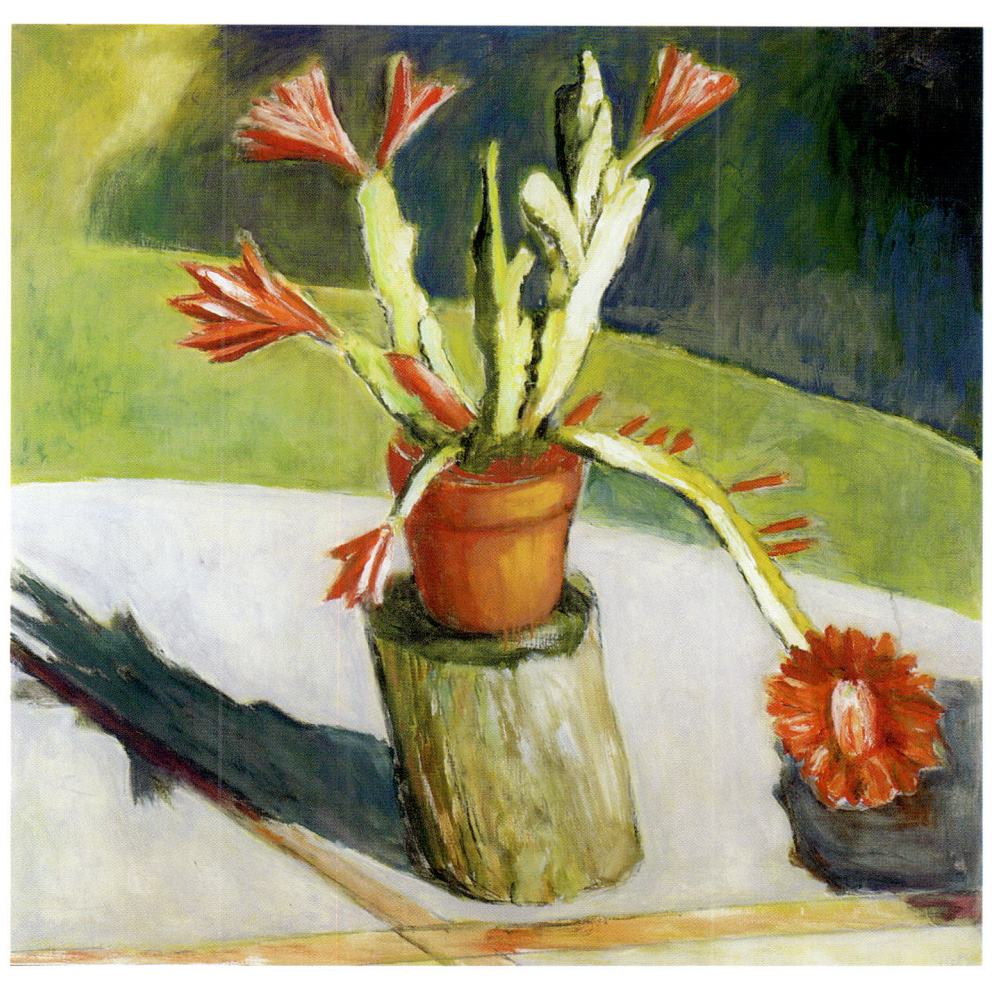

28 **toward morning**

march 1984

oil on canvas

48 x 60 inches

121.9 x 154.2 centimeters

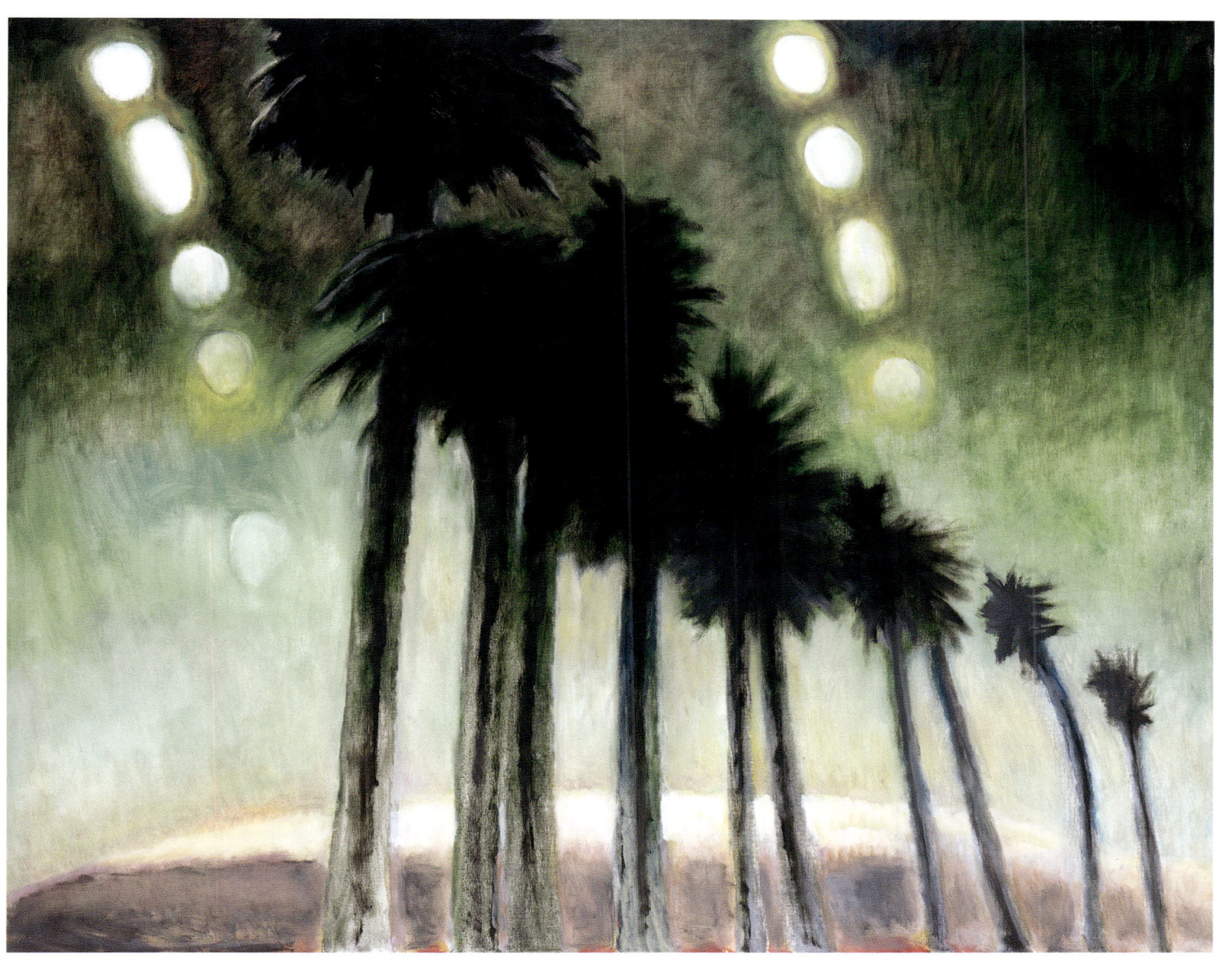

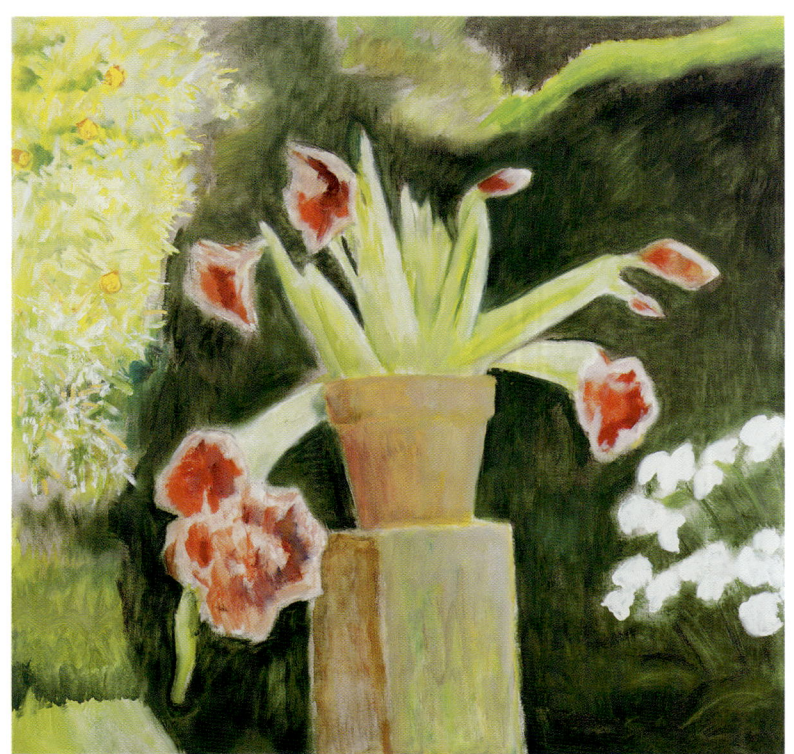

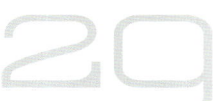 orchid cactus III

march 1984

oil on canvas

48 x 48 inches

121.9 x 121.9 centimeters

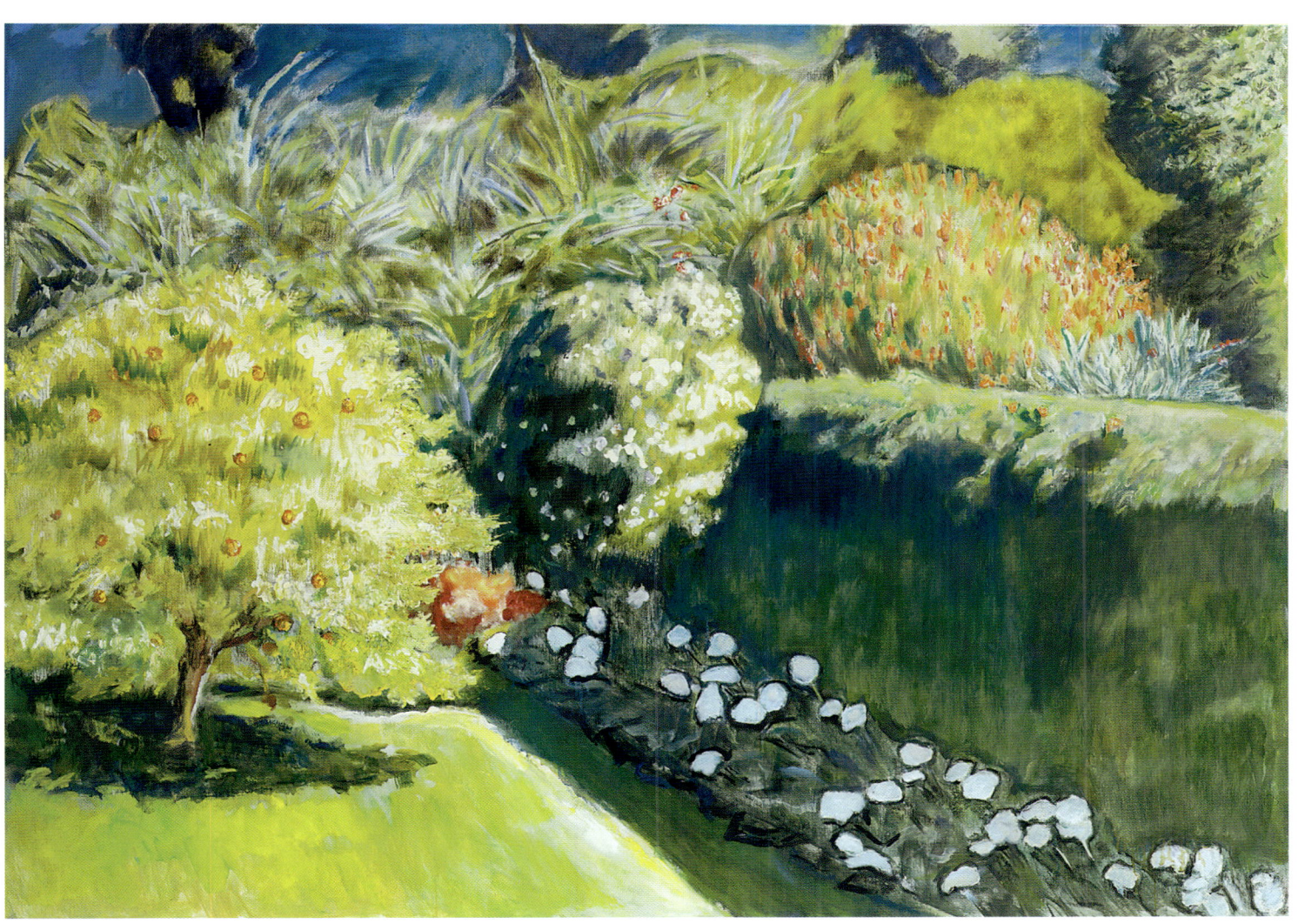

garden

april 1984

oil on canvas

48 x 66 inches

121.9 x 167.6 centimeters

31 plants on patio

may 1984

oil on canvas

32 x 22 inches

81.3 x 55.9 centimeters

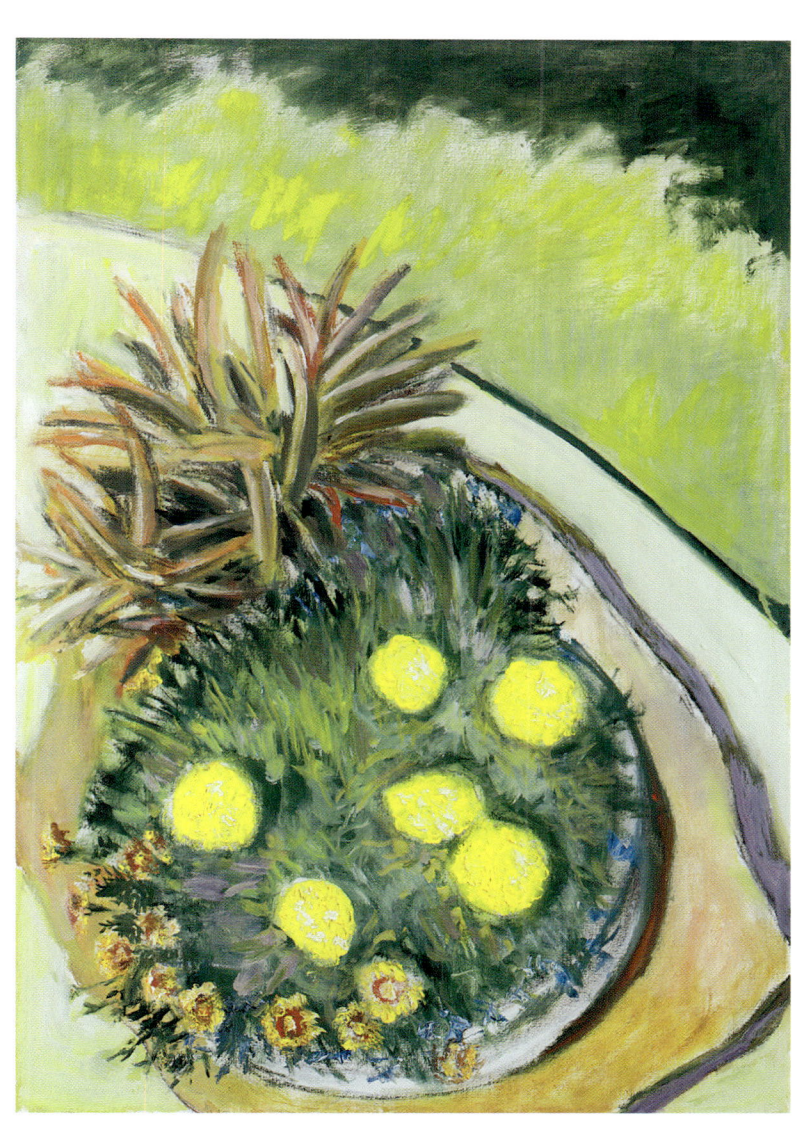

32 garden II

june 1984

oil on canvas

48 x 60 inches

121.9 x 154.2 centimeters

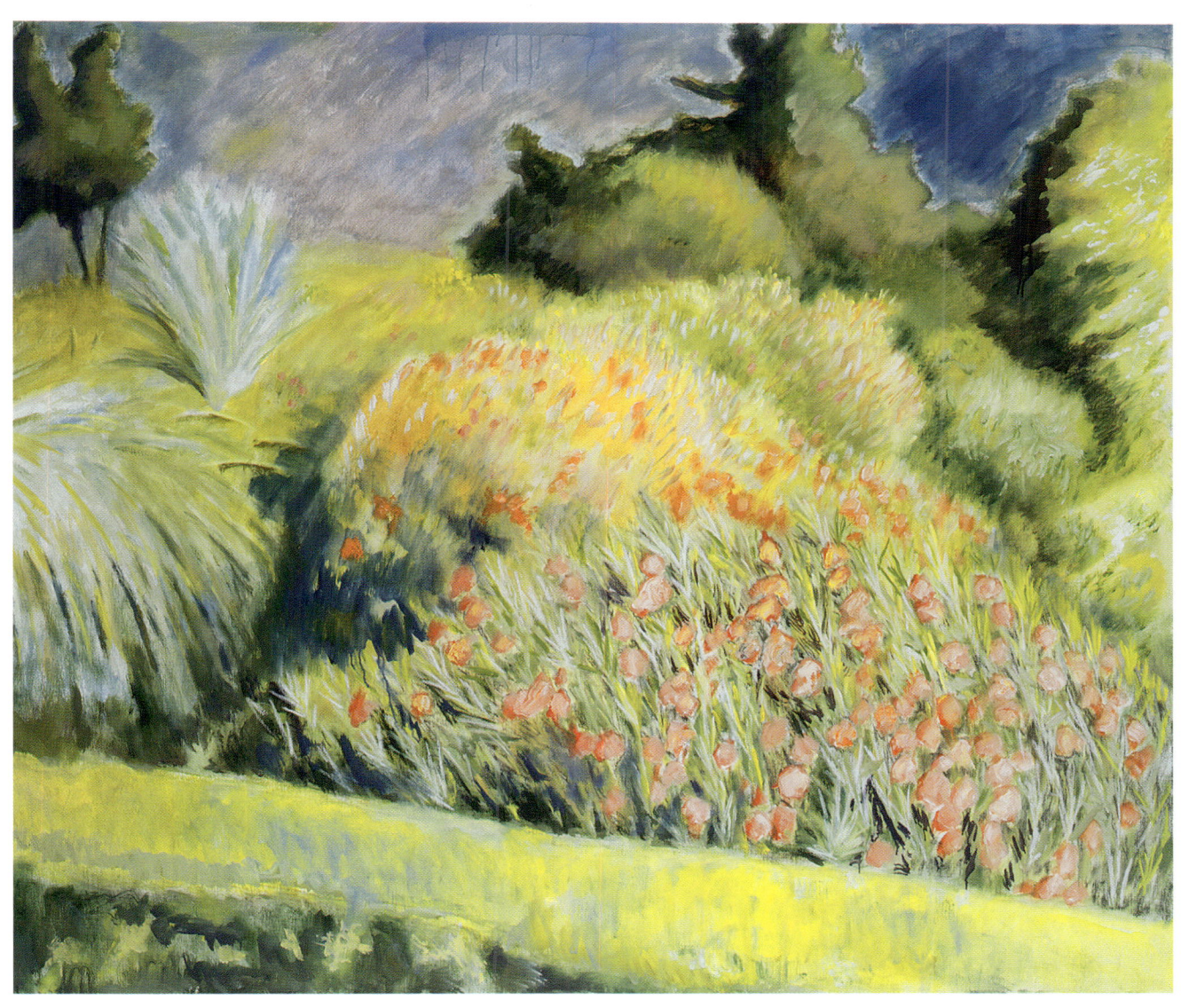

33 eclipse

july 1984

oil on canvas

30 x 48 inches

76.2 x 121.9 centimeters

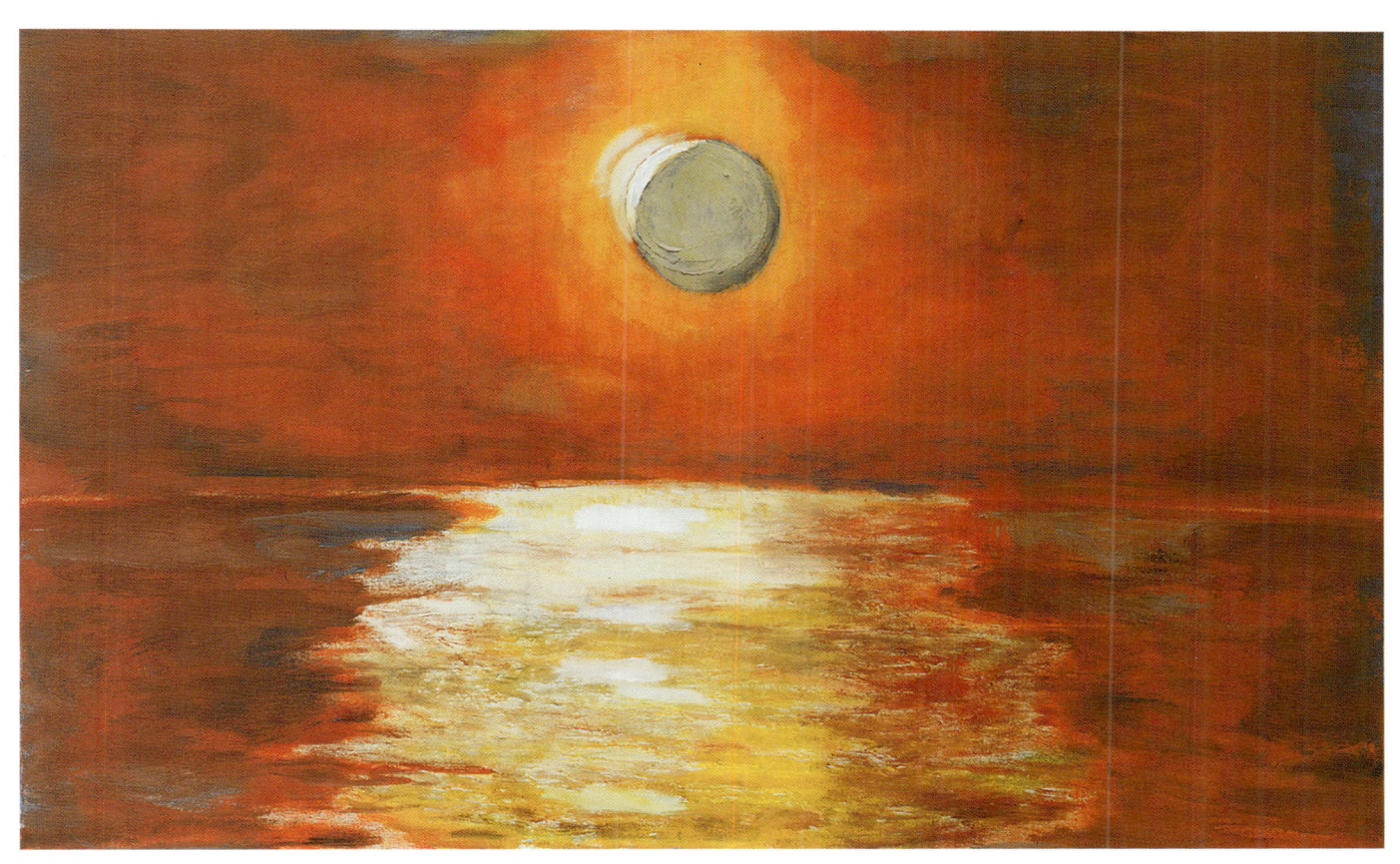

34 **meditation on mating**

november 1984

oil on canvas

48 x 54 inches

121.9 x 137.2 centimeters

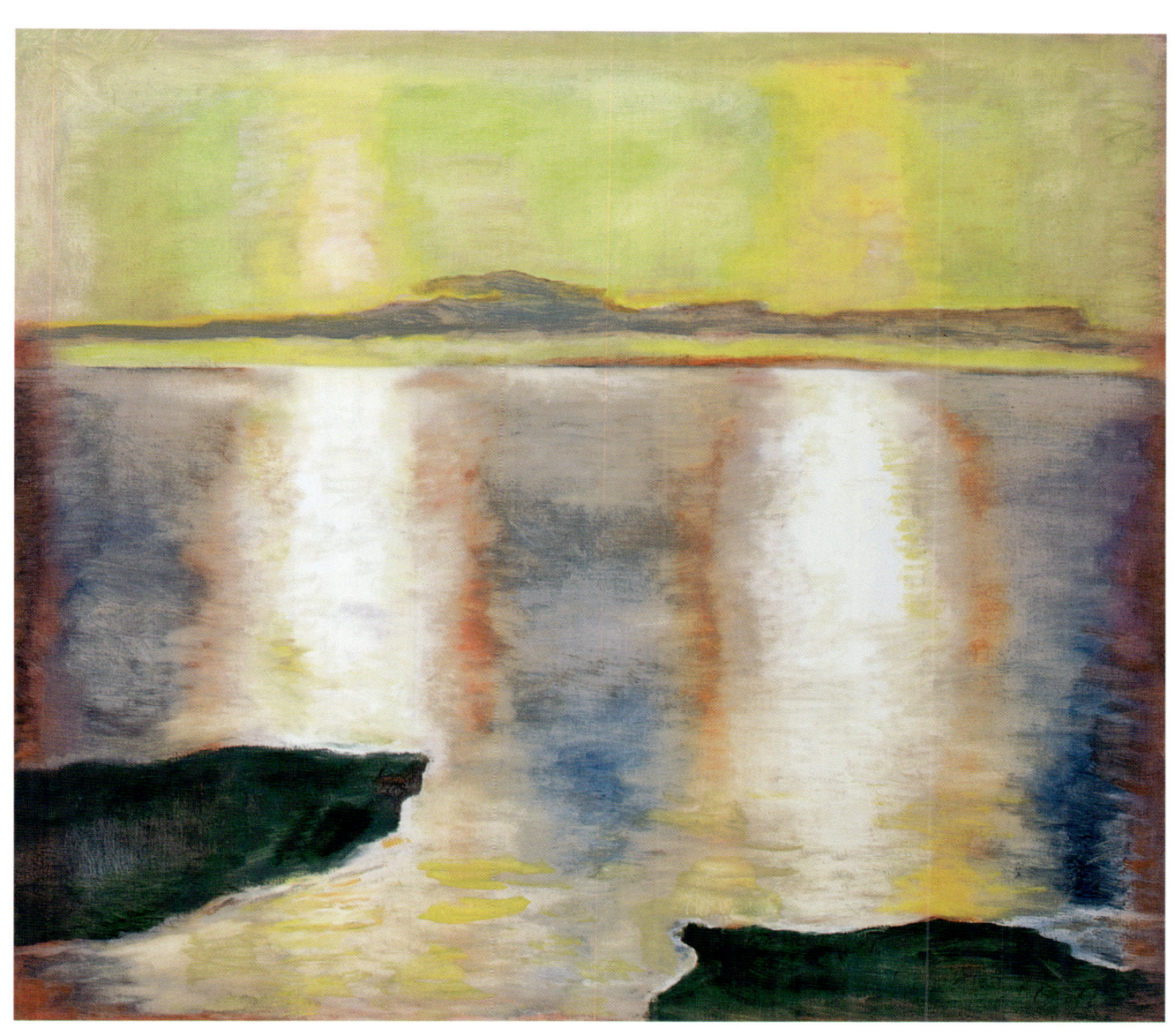

35 **school of clouds**

december 1984

oil on canvas

48 x 54 inches

121.9 x 137.2 centimeters

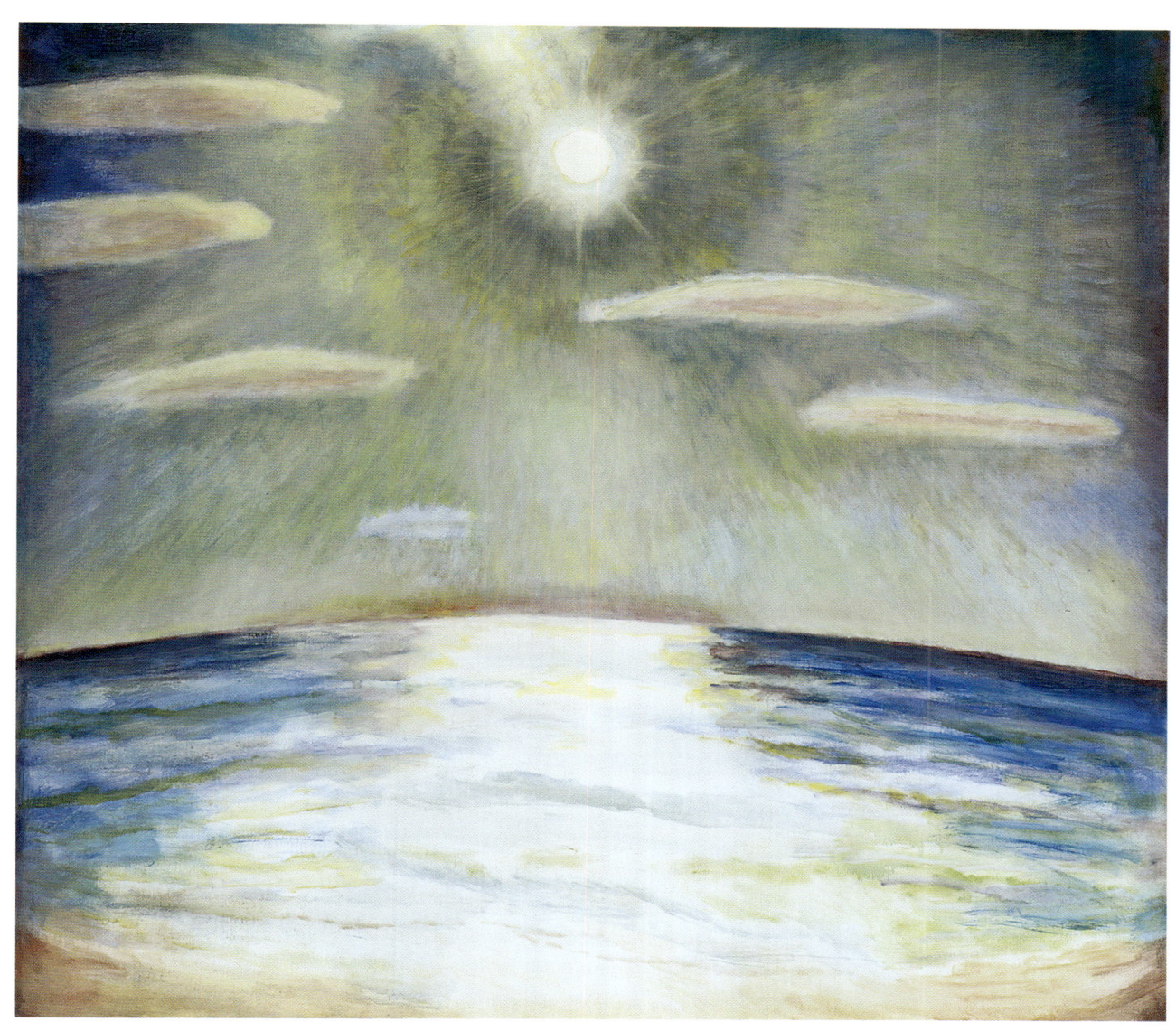

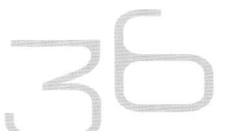

eight washingtonians
and three moons

july 1985

oil on canvas

48 x 72 inches

121.9 x 182.9 centimeters

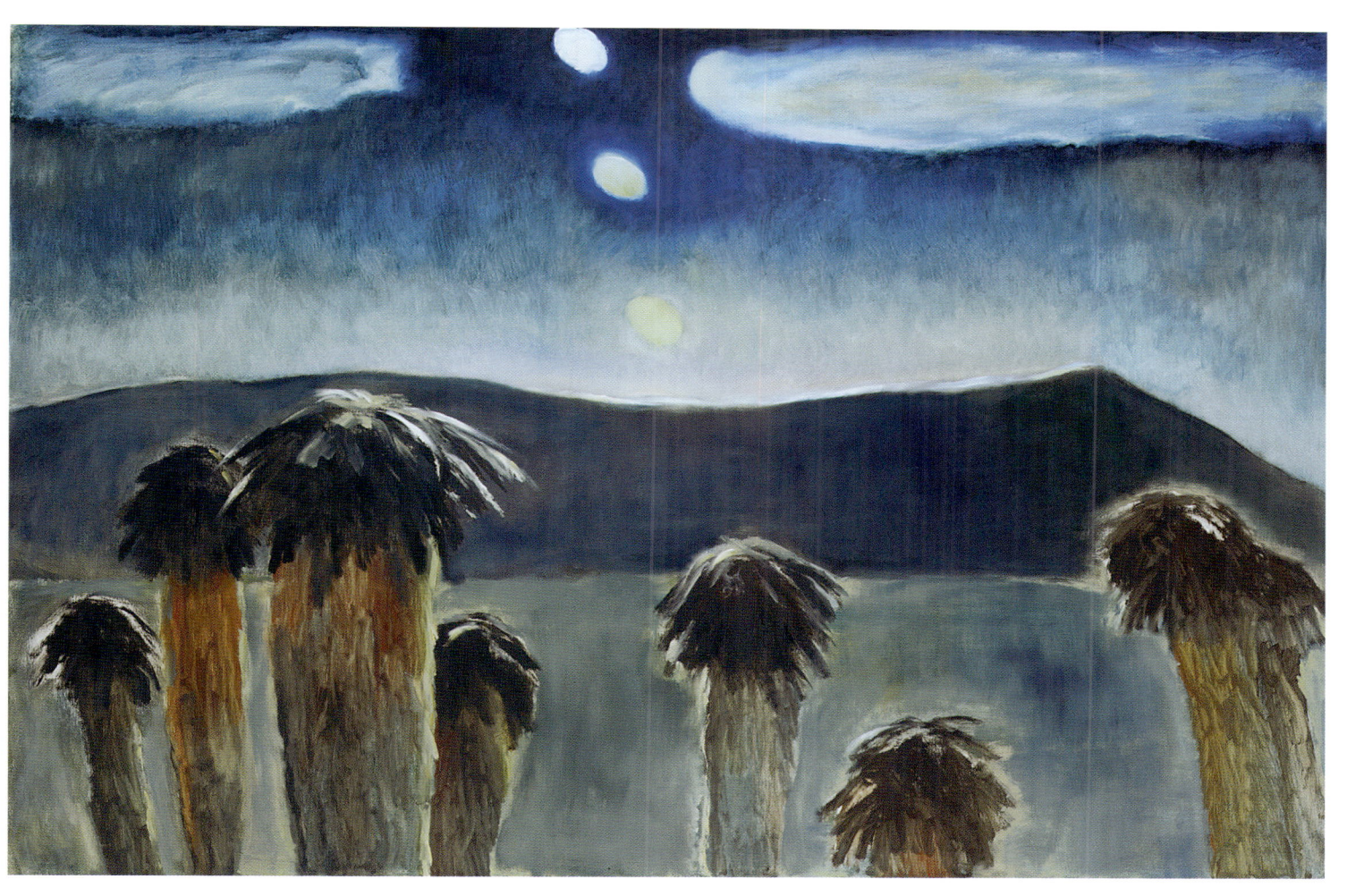

37 **washingtonians**

july 1985

oil on canvas

48 x 60 inches

121.9 x 152.4 centimeters

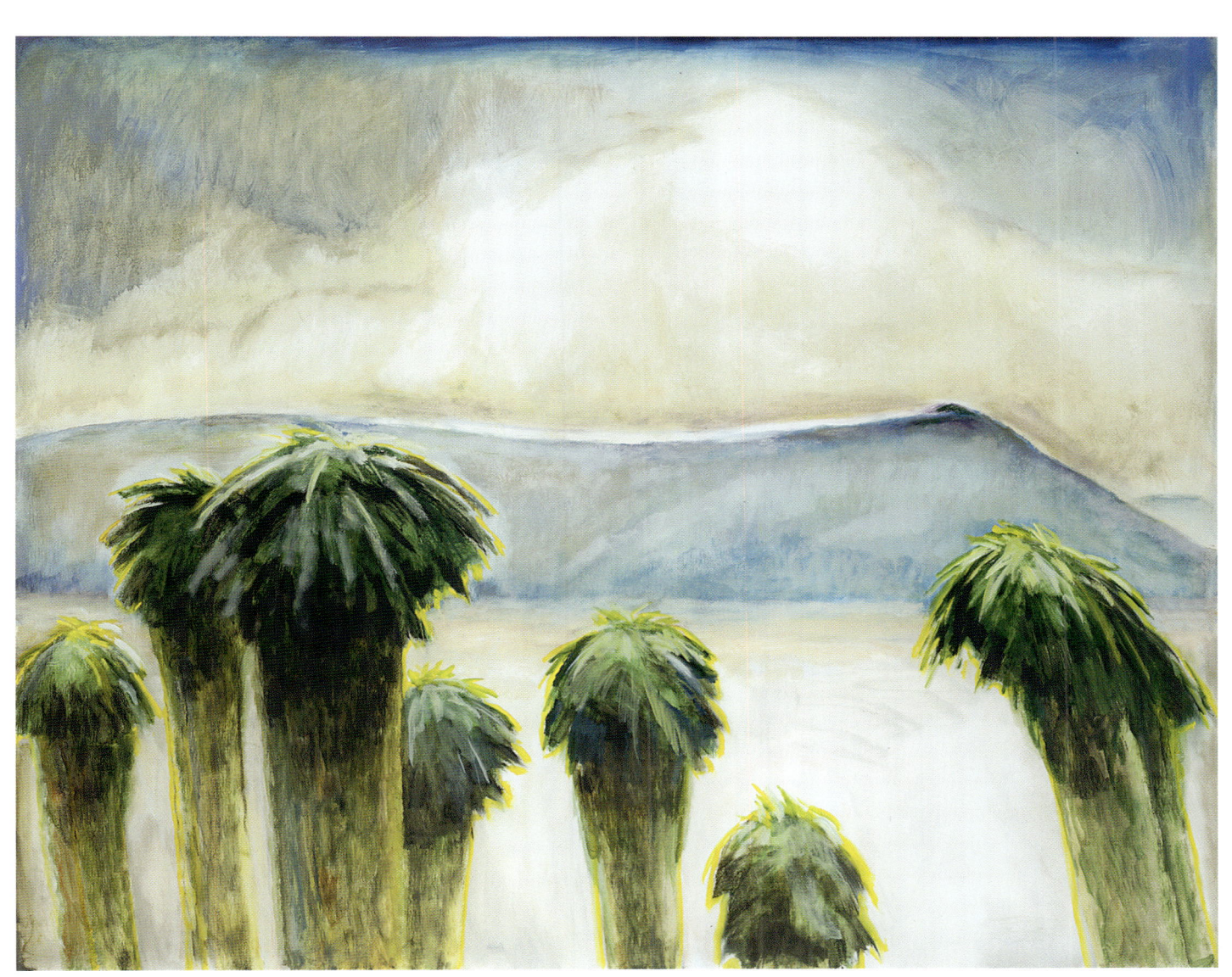

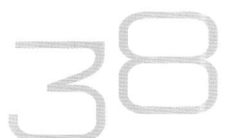 **mature palms**

february 1986

oil on canvas

48 x 66 inches

121.9 x 167.6 centimeters

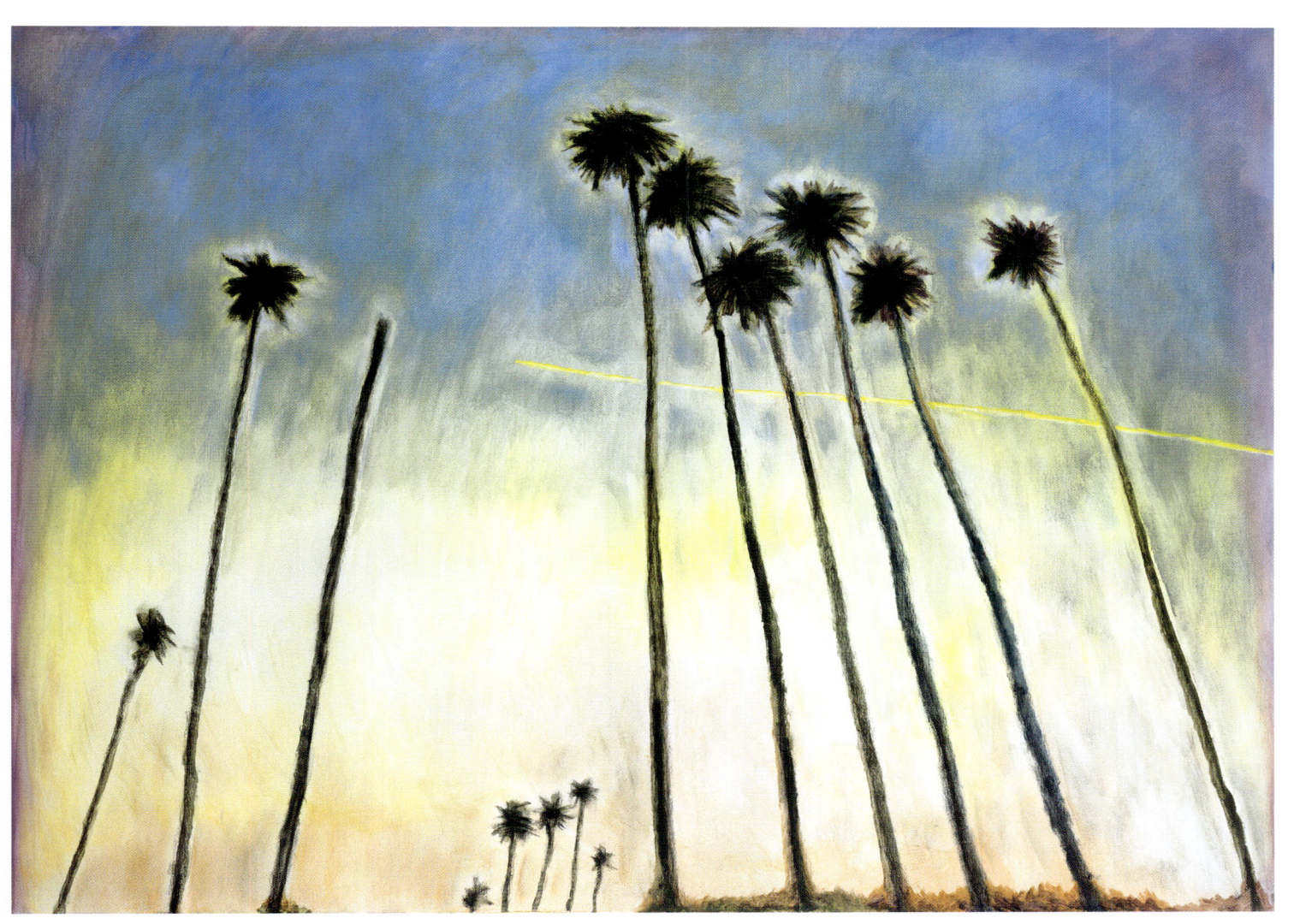

39 band

march 1986

oil on canvas

48 x 48 inches

121.9 x 121.9 centimeters

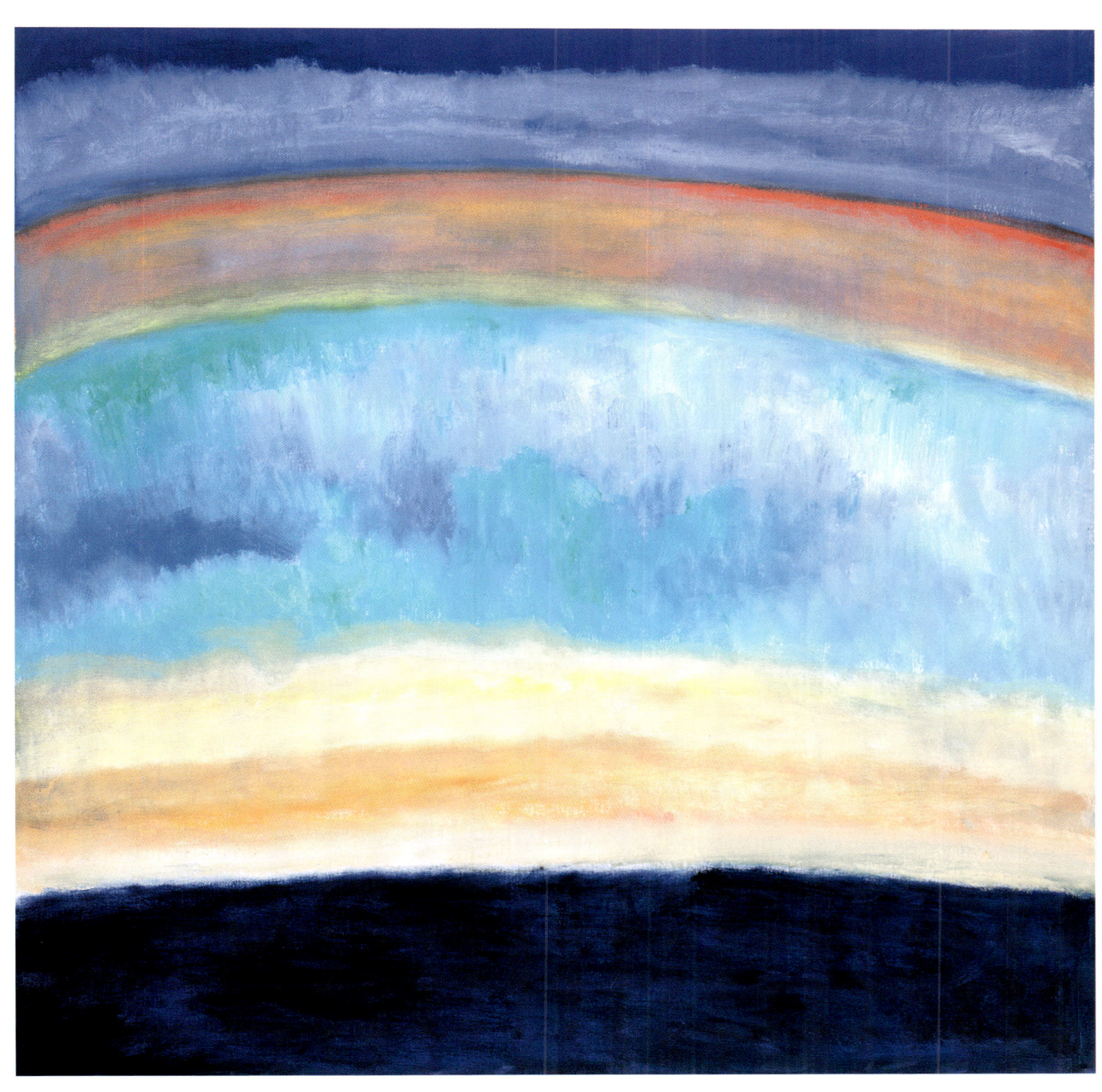

1902-1917

Born on June 1, 1902, in New York, New York, as the only child of Carol Wight and Alice Stallknect. The Wight Family moved throughout New York state and Vermont before settling in Chatham, Cape Cod, Massachusetts, in 1910. Frederick Wight entered high school in 1910, graduating at the age of fifteen.

1917-1925

Entered University of Virginia, completing his studies in 1923. After graduation he traveled to Paris to seriously pursue his artistic studies (his uncle, Dr. Sherman Wight, financed his endeavors). Studied at the Académie Julian from 1923-1925.

1925-1935

Returned to Cape Cod in 1925, where he painted portraits during most of the year and visited Virginia and Georgia during the winter in search of warmer climates. Occasional commissions furnished by Mrs. Cornelius Sullivan. Other subjects for portraits included: Eskine Caldwell, James Branch Campbell, and Edward Seidel Canby. Later portraits completed for Jacques Lipchitz and Lyonel Feininger, as well as local Cape Cod captains. First novel, *South*, published in 1935 to encouraging critical attention.

1936-1942

Marriage to Joan Elizabeth Bingham in 1936. The following two years were spent traveling in Joan's home country of England, and also to the south of France, which made a strong impression on Wight's art, resulting in several colorful landscape paintings. Passed through a brief experimental period, which he called "Semi-Surrealist." In 1938, Wight and Joan moved to Chatham, Massachusetts.

1942-1945

The couple's only child, George Frederick Wight, was born in Hyannis, Massachusetts, in 1942. Following onset of WWII, Frederick Wight joined the Navy and went overseas. He was initially hired as an illustrator but later became editor of the amphibious forces' newspaper based on his writing skills. Made drawing of Normandy beaches in preparation for the 1944 invasion landings, in which he later participated. Returned to London, where he worked for the Naval Division of Office of Strategic Services as an interrogator. After the capture of Paris, Wight was sent to the Continent to interview major Resistance leaders and to write an official American government report on the French resistance.

1945-1952

Wight is demobilized from the Navy in 1945 with the rank of lieutenant commander. He rejoined his family in Chatham and enrolled in Paul Sach's museum training program at Harvard's Fogg Art Museum, graduating with a Master's degree in 1946. Wrote principal essay for class' 1946 exhibition, *Between the Empires: Géricault, Delacroix, and Chassériau*, at the Fogg Art Museum. Worked with the following noted art historians: Agnes Mongan, John Rewald, and Jakob Rosenberg. After graduation, he was hired at Boston's Institute of Contemporary Art as director of education; later appointed to position of associate director of the Institute. Worked there 6 years, during which he mounted several important shows, including Louis Sullivan, José Clemente Orozco, Le Corbusier, and Walter Groupius.

1953-1973

Accepted a position as director of the new university Art Gallery at the University of California, Los Angeles, and also accepted a teaching position in the art department. Later served as department chairman. Shows hung during this period included *Bonne Fête, Monsieur Picasso*, *The Negro in American Art*, and *New British Painting and Sculpture*. Established the Art Council, a private support group of interested community members whose goal was to provide additional funding for the Art Gallery's programs. Directed the program for 2 decades. Other projects included the creation of the Franklin D. Murphy Sculpture Garden at UCLA and a residency spent at the American Academy at Rome in 1964.

1973-1986

In 1973, Wight retired from his position at UCLA. Upon his retirement, the University Art Gallery was renamed the Frederick S. Wight Art Gallery. His retirement allowed him to subsequently focus solely on his painting/artistic production. He died on July 26, 1986.

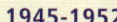

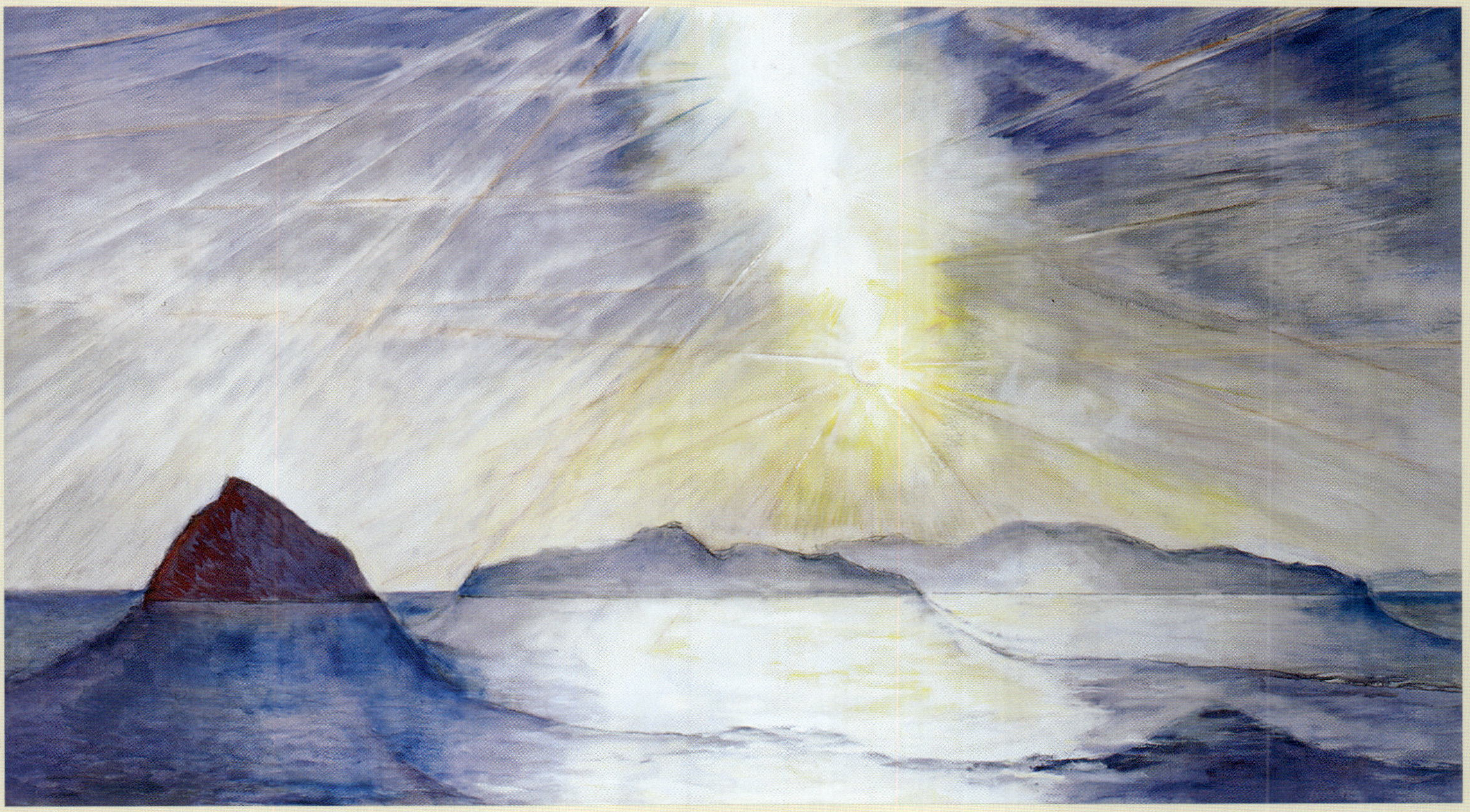

selected solo exhibitions

1956 *Paintings by Frederick S. Wight*, Pasadena Art Museum, Pasadena, California
1960 *Frederick Wight*, Esther Robles Gallery, Los Angeles, California
Roswell Museum, Roswell, New Mexico
University of New Mexico Galleries, Albuquerque, New Mexico
Museum of New Mexico Art Gallery, Santa Fe, New Mexico
1961 Long Beach Museum of Art. Long Beach, California
Palm Springs Desert Museum, Palm Springs, California
Frederick Wight: Paintings, Occidental College, Los Angeles, California
Colorado Springs Fine Arts Center, Colorado Springs, Colorado
1962 *New Paintings*, Esther Robles Gallery. Los Angeles, California
1963 Ankrum Gallery, Los Angeles, California
1964 Ankrum Gallery, Los Angeles, California
1965 Ankrum Gallery, Los Angeles, California
1966 Ankrum Gallery, Los Angeles, California
1967 Ankrum Gallery, Los Angeles, California
1968 *Frederick Wight*, Kovler Gallery, Chicago, Illinois
Frederick Wight, Ankrum Gallery, Los Angeles, California
1971 *Frederick Wight: Paintings and Extensions*, Ankrum Gallery, Los Angeles, California
1972 *Frederick Wight: Series 1972*, Ankrum Gallery, Los Angeles, California
1977 Stamford Museum and Nature Center, Stamford, Connecticut
1978 *Frederick Wight: Recent Paintings*, Palm Springs Desert Museum, Palm Springs, California
1981 *California Cycles*, Municipal Art Gallery at Barnsdall Park, Los Angeles, California
1982 *New Paintings*, Newspace, Los Angeles, California
1983 *Frederick Wight: Recent Work*, Galeries d'Art International, Chicago, Illinois
1984 *Paintings*, Newspace, Los Angeles, California
1985 *Frederick Wight*, Newspace, Los Angeles, California
1987 *The Last Paintings*, Newspace, Los Angeles, California
1989 *Gardens and Trees*, Newspace, Los Angeles, California
The Luminist Landscape, 871 Fine Arts, San Francisco, California
1990 *Sudden Nature: The Art of Frederick S. Wight 1902-1986*, UCLA Art Galleries, Los Angeles, California
1993 *Sun, Moon and Stars*, Newspace, Los Angeles, California
2000 *Painting Over Time*, Newspace, Los Angeles, California

selected group exhibitions

1982 *Les Americans de Paris*, Paris Art Center, Paris, France

The West As Art: Changing Perceptions of Western Art in California Collections, Palm Springs Desert Museum, Palm Springs, California

Cactus and Palms, The Downey Museum of Art, Downey, California

1983 *Florence Arnold and Frederick Wight*, Angeles Plaza, Los Angeles, California

1984 *There Is No Finish Line*, Newspace, Los Angeles, California

Selections from the Frederick R. Weisman Foundation at Mayor Tom Bradley's Office. City Hall, Los Angeles, California

1985 *Tenth Anniversary Thank You Show*, Newspace, Los Angeles, California

Landscape, Seascape, Cityscape, Contemporary Arts Center, New Orleans, Louisiana

Palms, Museum of Natural History, San Diego, California

To the Astonishing Horizon, LAVA IV, Design Center, Los Angeles, California

1986 *Dark Natures*, Newspace, Los Angeles, California

1987 *The Circle in Art*, Love Gallery, Chicago, Illinois

Nature, G.W. Einstein Gallery, New York, New York

Art in the Hall, West Hollywood City Hall, West Hollywood, California

The Great Outdoors: Selections From the Chemical Bank Art Collection, Chemical Gallery, New York, New York

1988 *Changing Visions: California Then and Now*, Pacific Bell, San Ramon, California

1991 *Alice and Fred*, Newspace, Los Angeles, California

1999 *The Decade Show: The Pasadena Art Museum 1949-1959 Revisited*, Mountain View Memorial Gallery, Altadena, California

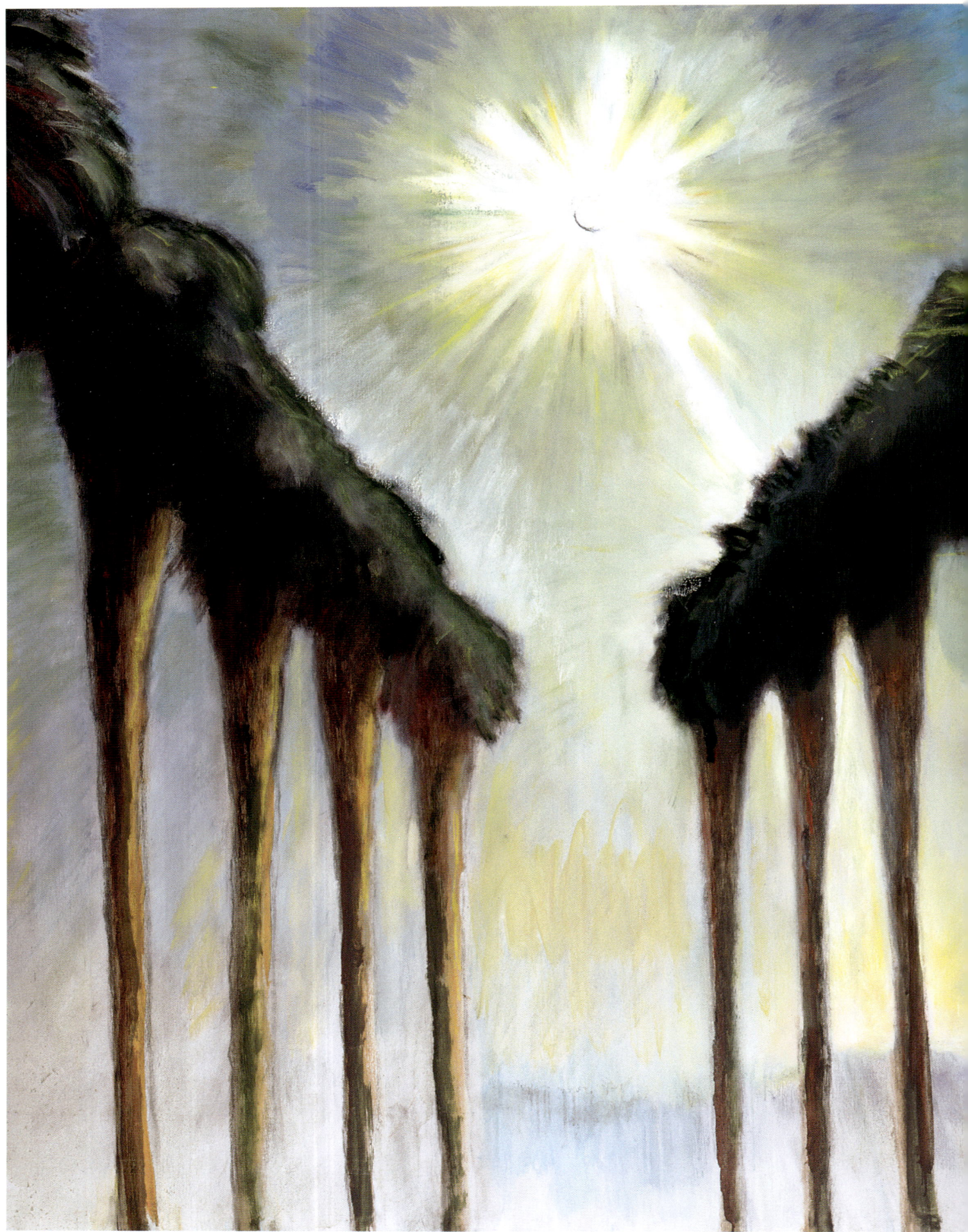

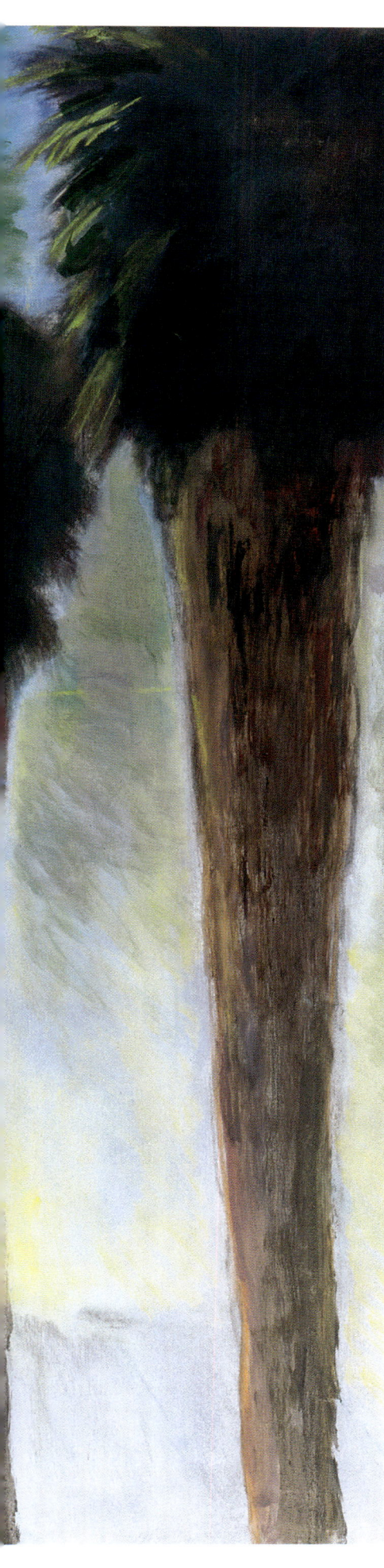

collections

selected private collections

Joe and Barbara Adler, Sherman Oaks, California
Martha Alf, Venice, California
Orlando Antonini, San Francisco, California
David Cason, Los Angeles, California
Dennis Dickinson, Los Angeles, California
Helen Epstein, Los Angeles, California
Joni and Monte Gordon, Los Angeles, California
Mr. and Mrs. John D. O'Donnell, San Francisco, California
Gae and Mel Shulman, San Francisco, California
Arnold Stiefel, Beverly Hills, California
Steve Sztopek, Los Angeles, California
Wayne Warga, Los Angeles, California
George Wight, Los Angeles, California

selected public collections

Chatham Historical Society, Chatham, Massachusetts
The Frederick R. Weisman Foundation, Los Angeles, California
Greenville County Art Museum, Greenville, North Carolina
Kaufman and Broad, Inc., Los Angeles, California
Laguna Art Museum, Laguna Beach, California
The Lannan Foundation, Los Angeles, California
Los Angeles County Museum of Art, Los Angeles, California
Newspace, Los Angeles, Los Angeles, California
Orange County Museum of Art, Newport Beach, California
Palm Springs Desert Museum, Palm Springs, California
Santa Barbara Museum of Art, Santa Barbara, California
Texas Commerce Bank, Dallas, Texas
UCLA Art Galleries, Los Angeles, California
Union Bank, Los Angeles, California
The Wight Trust, Los Angeles, California

1. **Three Palms**
   March 1975
   oil on canvas
   96 x 43 inches
   243.8 x 109.2 centimeters

2. **Orchid Catcus**
   December 1975
   oil on canvas
   30 x 15 inches
   76.2 x 38.1 centimeters

3. **Graptopetalum**
   December 1975
   oil on canvas
   48 x 33 inches
   121.9 x 83.8 centimeters

4. **San Gorgonio**
   May 1976
   oil on canvas
   49 x 54 inches
   124.5 x 137.2 centimeters

5. **Two Palms, Evening II**
   April 1977
   oil on canvas
   38 x 49 inches
   96.5 x 124.5 centimeters

6. **Palms Dusk**
   January 1978
   oil on canvas
   59 x 52 inches
   149.9 x 132.1 centimeters

7. **The Garden**
   May 1978
   oil on canvas
   96 x 48 inches
   243.9 x 121.9 centimeters

8. **The New Tree**
   January 1979
   oil on canvas
   96 x 51 inches
   243.9 x 129.5 centimeters

9. **Monte Rosa and Three Palms**
   January 1979
   oil on canvas
   51 x 59 inches
   129.5 x 149.9 centimeters

10. **Short Night**
    February 1979
    oil on canvas
    40 x 99 inches
    101.6 x 251.5 centimeters

11. **Morning Hours**
    June 1979
    oil on canvas
    72 x 50 inches
    182.9 x 127 centimeters

12. **Suddenly Afternoon**
    July 1979
    oil on canvas
    98 x 70 inches
    248.9 x 177.8 centimeters

13. **Succulent**
    April 1980
    oil on canvas
    29 x 22 inches
    73.7 x 55.9 centimeters

14. **Four Palms and a Mountain (Monte Rosa)**
    May 1980
    oil on canvas
    47 x 48 inches
    119.4 x 121.9 centimeters

15. **Entrance to the Ranch**
    August 1980
    oil on canvas
    51 x 73 inches
    129.5 x 185.4 centimeters

16. **Blue Islands**
    December 1980
    oil on canvas
    50 x 72 inches
    127 x 182.9 centimeters

17. **Desert Morning (Morning Hours II)**
    January 1981
    oil on canvas
    78 x 50 inches
    198.1 x 127 centimeters

18. **Tame Palms**
    March 1982
    oil on canvas
    36 x 40 inches
    91.4 x 101.6 centimeters

19. **Looking West**
    August 1982
    oil on canvas
    36 x 48 inches
    91.4 x 121.9 centimeters

20. **Returning Day**
    August 1982
    oil on canvas
    48 x 66 inches
    121.9 x 167.6 centimeters

21. **Santa Ana Blowing** (diptych)
    October 1982
    oil on canvas
    96 x 36 inches
    243.8 x 91.4 centimeters

exhibition checklist

22. **Midwinter**
    April 1983
    oil on canvas
    50 x 40 inches
    127 x 101.6 centimeters

23. **Midwinter II**
    April 1983
    oil on canvas
    48 x 48 inches
    121.9 x 121.9 centimeters

24. **Spring**
    May 1983
    oil on canvas
    48 x 48 inches
    121.9 x 121.9 centimeters

25. **Pacific**
    May 1983
    oil on canvas
    48 x 66 inches
    121.9 x 167.6 centimeters

26. **Six Palms**
    June 1983
    oil on canvas
    40 x 46 inches
    101.6 x 116.8 centimeters

27. **Orchid Cactus II**
    July 1983
    oil on canvas
    44 x 44 inches
    111.8 x 111.8 centimeters

28. **Toward Morning**
    March 1984
    oil on canvas
    48 x 60 inches
    121.9 x 154.2 centimeters

29. **Orchid Cactus III**
    March 1984
    oil on canvas
    48 x 48 inches
    121.9 x 121.9 centimeters

30. **Garden**
    April 1984
    oil on canvas
    48 x 66 inches
    121.9 x 167.6 centimeters

31. **Plants on Patio**
    May 1984
    oil on canvas
    32 x 22 inches
    81.3 x 55.9 centimeters

32. **Garden II**
    June 1984
    oil on canvas
    48 x 60 inches
    121.9 x 154.2 centimeters

33. **Eclipse**
    July 1984
    oil on canvas
    30 x 48 inches
    76.2 x 121.9 centimeters

34. **Meditation on Mating**
    November 1984
    oil on canvas
    48 x 54 inches
    121.9 x 137.2 centimeters

35. **School of Clouds**
    December 1984
    oil on canvas
    48 x 54 inches
    121.9 x 137.2 centimeters

36. **Eight Washingtonians
    and Three Moons**
    July 1985
    oil on canvas
    48 x 72 inches
    121.9 x 182.9 centimeters

37. **Washingtonians**
    July 1985
    oil on canvas
    48 x 60 inches
    121.9 x 152.4 centimeters

38. **Mature Palms**
    February 1986
    oil on canvas
    48 x 66 inches
    121.9 x 167.6 centimeters

39. **Band**
    March 1986
    oil on canvas
    48 x 48 inches
    121.9 x 121.9 centimeters

Chronology of selected publications and museum exhibitions

William Hayes Fogg Art Museum. *Between the Empires: Géricault, Delacroix, Chassériau: Painters of the Romantic Movement.* Cambridge, Massachusetts: Harvard University Printing Office, 1946. (Essay by Frederick S. Wight.)

William Hayes Fogg Art Museum. *French Painting Since 1870.* Cambridge, Massachusetts: Harvard University Painting Office, 1946. (Entries by Frederick S. Wight.)

The Institute of Contemporary Art. *Le Corbusier: New World of Space.* Exhibition catalogue. New York: Reynal and Hitchcock and the Institute of Contemporary Art, 1948.

The Institute of Contemporary Art. *Jacques Villon—Lyonel Feininger.* Exhibition catalogue. New York: Chanticleer Press, n.d. [1949 or 1950]

Wight, Frederick S. *Milestones of American Painting in Our Century.* Exhibition catalogue. The Institute of Contemporary Art. New York: Chanticleer Press, 1949.

The Institute of Contemporary Art. *Karl Zerbe.* Exhibition catalogue. Boston: The Institute of Contemporary Art. n.d.

The Cleveland Museum of Art. *The Work of Lyonel Feininger.* Exhibition catalogue. The Cleveland Museum of Art, 1951. (Essay by Frederick S. Wight.)

Wight. Frederick S. *Chrysalis: Six American Painters.* Exhibition catalogue. Boston: Institute of Contemporary Art, 1951, volume 4, numbers 3-4.

Baltimore Museum of Art. *Milton Avery.* Exhibition catalogue. Baltimore: Baltimore Museum of Art, 1952.

The Institute of Contemporary Art. *Hyman Bloom.* Exhibition catalogue. Boston: The Institute of Contemporary Art, 1954.

The UCLA Art Galleries. *Charles Sheeler: A Retrospective Exhibition.* Exhibition catalogue. Los Angeles: The UCLA Art Galleries, 1954.

Wight, Frederick S. *Goya.* New York: Harry N. Abrams, 1954.

The UCLA Art Galleries. *John Marin Memorial Exhibition.* Exhibition catalogue. Los Angeles: University of California, 1955.

Contemporary Arts Museum. *Contemporary Calligraphers: John Marin, Mark Tobey, Morris Graves.* Exhibition catalogue. Houston: Contemporary Arts Museum, 1956. (Forward by Frederick S. Wight.)

The UCLA Art Galleries. *Morris Graves.* Exhibition catalogue. Los Angeles: The Regents of the University of California, 1956.

The UCLA Art Galleries. *Hans Hoffmann.* Exhibition catalogue. Los Angeles: The Regents of the University of California, 1957.

The UCLA Art Galleries. *Arthur G. Dove.* Exhibition catalogue. Los Angeles: The Regents of the University of California, 1958.

The UCLA Art Galleries. *Richard Neutra.* Exhibition catalogue. Los Angeles: The Regents of the University of California, 1958.

Los Angeles County Museum of Art and Museum of Fine Arts, Boston. *Modigliani: Paintings and Drawings.* Exhibition catalogue. Los Angeles: The Committee on Fine Arts Productions. University of California, Los Angeles, 1961.

The UCLA Art Galleries. *Bonne Fête, Monsieur Picasso.* Los Angeles: The Committee on Fine Arts Production. University of California, Los Angeles, 1961.

The UCLA Art Galleries. *French Masters: Rococo to Romanticism.* Exhibition catalogue. Los Angeles: The UCLA Art Galleries, 1961.

The Amon Carter Museum of Western Art. *The Artist's Environment: West Coast.* Exhibition catalogue. Fort Worth: The Amon Carter Museum of Western Art, 1962.

The UCLA Art Galleries. *Lithographs from the Tamarind Workshop.* Exhibition catalogue. Los Angeles: The UCLA Art Galleries, 1962.

The UCLA Art Galleries. *The Gifford and Joann Phillips Collection.* Exhibition catalogue. Los Angeles: The UCLA Art Galleries, 1962. (Introduction by Frederick S. Wight.)

The Pavilion Gallery. *Morris Graves.* Exhibition catalogue. Balboa, California: Fine Arts Patrons of Newport Harbor and Newport Harbor Service League, 1963.

The UCLA Art Galleries. *Jacques Lipchitz.* Exhibition catalogue. Los Angeles: The UCLA Art Galleries, 1963.

The UCLA Art Galleries. *Nathan Oliveira.* Exhibition catalogue. Los Angeles: The UCLA Art Galleries, 1963.

Fine Arts Patrons of Newport Harbor. *Rico Lebrun.* Exhibition catalogue. Newport Harbor, California: Fine Arts Patrons, Newport Pavilion Gallery, 1964.

The UCLA Art Galleries. *From the Ludington Collection.* Exhibition catalogue. Los Angeles: The UCLA Art Galleries, 1964.

selected bibliography

The UCLA Art Galleries. *Years of Ferment: The Birth of Twentieth Century Art: 1886-1914*. Exhibition catalogue. Los Angeles: The UCLA Art Galleries, 1965. (Forward by Frederick S. Wight.)

The UCLA Art Galleries. *Henri Matisse*. Exhibition catalogue. Los Angeles: UCLA Art Council and the UCLA Art Galleries, 1966.

The UCLA Art Galleries. *The Negro in American Art*. Exhibition catalogue. Los Angeles: The UCLA Art Galleries, 1966.

The UCLA Art Galleries. *Alexander Archipenko*. Exhibition catalogue. Los Angeles: The Regents of the University of California, 1967.

The UCLA Art Galleries. *Arp Memorial Exhibition*, 1968. (Exhibition organized in conjunction with the publication of Herbert Read, *Jean Arp*, New York: Harry N. Abrams, 1968.)

The Whitechapel Gallery. *New British Painting and Sculpture*. Exhibition catalogue. London: The Whitechapel Gallery, 1968.

The UCLA Art Galleries. *Electric Art*. Exhibition catalogue. Los Angeles: The UCLA Art Galleries, 1969.

The UCLA Art Galleries. *Gerhard Marcks*. Exhibition catalogue. Los Angeles: The UCLA Art Galleries, 1969.

The UCLA Art Galleries. *Color*. Exhibition catalogue. Los Angeles: The UCLA Art Galleries, n.d. [1970]. (Organized as part of an Art Department graduate seminar under the direction of Frederick S. Wight.)

The UCLA Art Galleries and the Grunwald Graphic Arts Foundation. *Stanton MacDonald-Wright: A Retrospective Exhibition*. Exhibition catalogue. Los Angeles: The UCLA Art Galleries and the Grunwald Graphic Arts Foundation, 1970.

The UCLA Art Galleries. *Deliberate Engagements*. Exhibition catalogue. Los Angeles: The UCLA Art Galleries, 1971. (Preface by Frederick S. Wight.)

The UCLA Art Galleries. *Transparency, Reflection, Light, Space: Four Artists*. Exhibition catalogue. Los Angeles: The UCLA Art Galleries, 1971.

The UCLA Art Galleries. *Twentieth Century Sculpture from Southern California Collections*. Exhibition catalogue. Los Angeles: The UCLA Art Galleries, 1972.

Wight, Frederick S. *The Potent Image: Art in the Western World from Cave Paintings to the 1970s*. New York: Collier Books, Division of Macmillan Publishing Inc., 1976.

Galleries of the Claremont Colleges. *Works on Paper 1900-1960 from Southern California Collections*. Exhibition catalogue. Pomona: Galleries of the Claremont Colleges, 1977. (Introduction by Frederick S. Wight.)

Novels

Wight, Frederick S. *South*. New York: Farrar and Rinehart, Inc., 1935.

Wight, Frederick S. *The Chronicle of Aaron Kane*. New York: Farrar and Rinehart, Inc., 1936.

Wight, Frederick S. *Youth in Trust*. New York and Toronto: Farrar and Rinehart Inc., 1937.

Wight, Frederick S. *Inner Harbor*. Boston: Little, Brown, and Company, 1949.

Wight, Frederick S. *Kindling*. Boston: Little, Brown, and Company, 1951.

Wight, Frederick S. *Verge of Glory*. New York: Harcourt Brace and Company, 1956.

Front Cover: *Toward Morning*, detail (Plate 28)

Back Cover: *Succulent*, (Plate 13)

Page 15: Photograph of the artist by Karen Wight

Photography by Ed Glendinning

Design: Lilla Hangay, Santa Ana, CA
Production: Color West Inc., Burbank, CA
Typeface: Diphtong, Frutiger
Printed on Topkote dull
Edition of 7000

© Text by Henry T. Hopkins
© Essay by Susan C. Larsen

All rights reserved. No part of this catalogue may be reproduced in any form by any electronic or mechanical means (including photocopying, recording, or information storage and retrieval) without permission in writing from the publisher.

© 2005 Louis Stern Fine Arts, 9002 Melrose Avenue, West Hollywood, CA 90069

ISBN 0-9749421-2-X
Library of Congress Control Number: 2005924004

Printed in U.S.A.